Raymond Sanchez Mayers, PhD, is the author of *Financial Management for Nonprofit Human Service Agencies* and other works. He is currently Associate Professor at the School of Social Work, Rutgers University.

Federico Souflee, Jr., PhD, is the co-author of *Human Services Management* and other works. He is currently Assistant Professor at the School of Social Work, University of Texas at Arlington.

Dick J. Schoech, PhD, is the author of *Computer Use in Human Services* and numerous other works related to computers and management. He is currently Professor at the School of Social Work, University of Texas at Arlington.

Dilemmas in Human Services Management

Illustrative Case Studies

Raymond Sanchez Mayers, PhD

Federico Souflee, Jr, PhD

Dick J. Schoech, PhD

Springer Publishing Company
New York

Springer Publishing Company, Inc.
536 Broadway
New York, NY 10012

Cover and interior design by Holly Block

01 02 / 7 6

Library of Congress Cataloging-in-Publication Data

Mayers, Raymond Sanchez.
  Dilemmas in human services management: Illustrative case studies/ Raymond Sanchez Mayers, Federico Souflee, Jr., Dick J. Schoech.
    p. cm. — (Springer series on social work)
  Includes bibliographical references and index.
  ISBN 0-8261-7740-9
    1. Human services—United States—Management—Case studies.
  2. Human services—United States—Administration—Case studies.
  I. Souflee, Federico. II. Schoech, Dick. III. Title. IV. Series:
  Springer series on social work.
  HV91.M374   1994
  361'.0068—dc20   93-50540
                                                                CIP

Printed in the United States of America

For
Carann, Sara Caitlin, and Jordan
Norma
Sharon

Contents

A Budget Cut

Board / Staff Role
Herb Goldberg Case
Union Case

Mission
Vision
Governance

Preface

As teachers of management for social work students, we are acutely aware of the difficulty in teaching the skills-based components of an administration curriculum. We know that students need to develop skills that can be transferred to the workplace. Developing complex skills needed for effective management is difficult in the classroom situation. This is one reason the field internship is so important. However, many times field work is not taken in conjunction with required administration classes or students are not afforded the broad range of experiences necessary to develop expertise in, or even familiarity with, certain areas. That is why we developed this casebook.

This book is composed of short cases on aspects of human service administration. It is designed to be used in courses in social work administration, human service or non-profit management, and other similar courses as a supplement to a good human services management textbook. Its purpose is to provide students with an opportunity to apply management concepts to simulated "real life" problems and issues.

The case method has been found to be a very effective way of having students demonstrate acquisition of knowledge and skill by having them apply concepts to situations and describe how they would resolve the problems. (See Chapter 2 for a further discussion of the use of the case method.) Each case provides an overview of the setting in which the action occurs, a profile of the key actors involved, and other information needed by the student in order to make decisions, and to demonstrate mastery of a concept. At the end of each case, the student may use the guidelines given in Chapter Two as the basis for a paper, presentation, or discussion. Using these guidelines, the student is asked to assume that she/he is a manager who must make critical decisions regarding the issues involved.

Some unique aspects of this book are the following.

Cases Address Human Service Issues

All of the cases in this book try to address the unique character of human service agencies, both public and private. Although certain types of problems appear common to most organizations, these cases place them within the context of the human service agency with its mix of lay volunteers, human service professionals, interdisciplinary teams, complex array of funding sources, and myriad state, federal, and local regulations and guidelines.

Flexibility in Analysis

We do not presume that there is only one way to address a problem. Therefore we have tried to offer flexibility to the instructor in letting him/her decide on a preferred method. Chapter 2 provides a framework and guidelines for the students to follow in reading and using the cases. The guidelines help students walk through the decision-making process, forcing them to look at factors and alternatives, and to develop logical rationales for their decisions. However, if the instructor chooses not to use the guidelines, each case has questions at the end that when answered, force students to consider the issues of each case.

Brevity of Cases

We have purposely developed short cases that can be read and answered relatively quickly by students as either in-class or homework assignments. The advantages of these short cases are that they do not require an inordinate amount of class time, but they do provide a very good basis for class discussion. Because they are short, they can cover most of the topics of an overview administration/planning course. This is especially important where students might not have any experience in areas such as supervision and working with boards.

Variety of Cases

We have endeavored to present a broad range of situations that a human service administrator might be exposed to in the course of his/her career. The cases are also presented from many different levels, that is, that of a first-line supervisor, a program director, as well as an executive director. This variety exposes the student to many of the problems faced at these different levels.

ORGANIZATION OF THE BOOK

Some management areas covered in this text include: planning, personnel issues, supervision, management information systems, interpersonal and intraorganizational conflict, board/staff relations, interorganizational relations, organizational change, organizational structure, grievance procedures, program evaluation, line/staff relations, sexual harassment, sexism, racism, affirmative action, and so forth (see Chapter One).

We have also provided an index listing of cases by topical area to make it easier for the reader to find a particular type of case.

Acknowledgments

The authors would like to thank all those who gave insightful comments about these cases, especially those graduate social work students in our administration/planning classes. We also appreciate the feedback we received from Dr. Mark Ezell and Dr. Al Roberts. Dr. Mayers would particularly like to acknowledge the assistance of two experienced human service administrators, Carann Simpson Feazell and Fontaine H. Fulghum, who not only gave of their time, but helped give these cases a reality check. Ms. Fulghum contributed one of the cases, "Planning and the Politics of Inclusion." Both read the manuscript numerous times and gave constructive suggestions.

❧ *Chapter One*

Human Services Management in Perspective

The management of human services has been described from a number of perspectives. Miringoff (1980) conceptualizes management as a system of interacting parts aimed at effective and efficient provision of services. Patti (1983), by contrast, sees management as consisting of six principal tasks with corresponding activities necessary for their accomplishment. These tasks are: planning and developing the program; acquiring financial resources and support; designing organizational structures and processes; developing and maintaining staff capability; assessing agency programs; and changing agency programs. Abels and Murphy (1981) take a somewhat different approach. They identify four key management functions around which decision making takes place. The functions are: planning, organizing, controlling, and motivating. Skidmore (1983) includes these functions in his listing of the elements of management, but adds the following: financial management, evaluation, leadership, communication, community relations, staffing, supervision, and staff development.

The management perspective adopted for purposes of this book is based, in large measure, on the human service management model developed by Lewis, Lewis, and Souflee (1991). This model, in modified form, includes all of the functions and tasks mentioned above. Like Miringoff (1980), the model is based on a systems perspective of management, and contains a set of interacting and interdependent components operating synergistically to produce program efficiency and effectiveness. The intent of this chapter is to discuss the

1

model and the ingredients of each of its components. Case illustrations, subsequently presented, relate to one or more of the components of the model.

THE HUMAN SERVICES MANAGEMENT MODEL

The elements of the model consist of discrete components which comprise the functions, processes, tasks, and activities of a comprehensive human services management system. These components are presented as sequential steps designed to be followed in the development of new programs within existing human service organizations, or in the creation of new agencies. Furthermore, the components can also be a part of everyday managerial operations in stable agencies not faced with the challenges of program expansion. In such instances, the interaction and interdependence between components may have reached a steady state requiring relatively routine kinetic activity among them. For present purposes, the model is presented in terms of the development of a new program within an existing agency.

Leadership is at the core of the management of human service programs, and is therefore accorded a central role in this human services management model. Although numerous variables affect organizational behavior, administrative leadership has long been recognized as a correlate of organizational effectiveness (Selznick, 1957; Etzioni, 1964; Miringoff, 1980; Perlmutter & Slavin, 1980; Abels & Murphy, 1981; Patti, 1983; Skidmore, 1983). This is not to say, however, that leadership is the only variable associated with effectiveness; it is simply to say that it is a vitally important one. Leadership lends coherence and direction to the other elements of the managerial process, as depicted in Figure 1 below. These components consist of strategic and tactical planning; the design of organizational structure; the establishment of technological rationality; resource procurement and allocation; coordination and control of program operations; program implementation; and program evaluation (see Figure 1.1).

As previously stated, there are many ways of conceptualizing the management of human service programs. The model depicted by Figure 1 is one of them. It is presented for purposes of providing the reader with a framework for the placement of case illustration within the management process. Since this is not a text on manage-

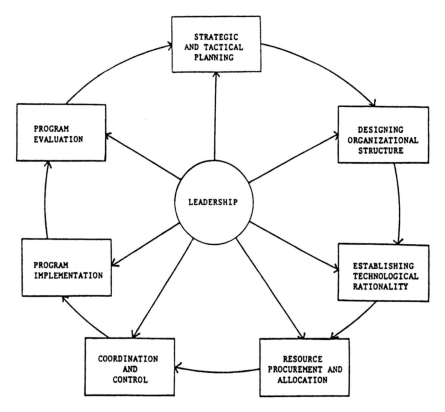

Figure 1.1. Human Services Management Model

ment per se, each of the components of the model is discussed in brief terms. It is assumed that readers have already undertaken or are currently engaged in a more in-depth examination of the elements of management than is herein presented.

Leadership

Leadership is one of the most studied and debated topics in the literature on organizational behavior. Consequently, perspectives on and definitions of leadership abound. In the present model, leadership is defined as the formal authority and responsibility conferred on one or more members of the organization to assure the achievement of organizational mission, goals, and objectives. This is not to ignore the existence and importance of informal leaders in organization; rather, it is to say that the focus is on positional leaders. Evans (1979) refers to the latter as appointed leaders, and the former as emergent leaders, and makes the following distinction between the two:

> [Appointed leaders] are defined as occupants of organizational roles (executive, manager, supervisor, lead hand) whose job descriptions require them to perform the managerial functions [of the enterprise]. [Emergent leaders] may or may not occupy formal positions of authority; they are usually selected because of the respect they enjoy in terms of getting the task done and/or maintaining the social fabric of the group. . . . (p. 212)

The leadership function, as conceptualized within the context of the model, is based on three assumptions. The first is that leadership is a shared function in human service organizations, starting with the dominant coalition, the chief executive officer, and extending to frontline supervisors. The second is that an efficient manager does not necessarily make an effective leader, and vice-versa. The third assumption is that, under ideal circumstances, persons in managerial positions in human service organizations should be both efficient managers and effective leaders in order to maximize efficient and effective program outcomes.

The first assumption—that leadership is a shared function—is premised on a hierarchical differentiation of positional authority and power. That is, whereas the dominant coalition may have the power and authority to formulate agency policies, the front-line supervisor's power and authority may be limited to the implementation of those policies. The degree of involvement of lower-echelon staff in policy formulation will reflect the degree to which the organization is centralized or decentralized.

The second assumption—that efficient management is not synonymous with effective leadership—speaks to the different knowledge and skills required of each role: whereas competent management is based on the mastery of technical knowledge and skills, competent leadership relies on the ability to influence others to achieve particular goals (Lewis, Lewis, & Souflee, 1991). At the executive level of the organization, leadership also requires, as Selznick (1957) observed, a broadened vision of the organization and its place in society. The executive becomes a statesman as he makes the transition from administrative management to institutional leadership. This shift entails a reassessment of his own tasks and of the needs of the enterprise. It is marked by a concern for the evolution of the organization as a whole, including its changing aims and capabilities. It means viewing the organization as an institution. For an organization to become institutionalized, it must be "infused with value," not just by its members, but by its environment as well. For both Barnard (1968) and Selznick (1957), the primary role of the institutional leader is to manage, promote, and protect the values of the organization.

The Human Services Management Model depicted in Figure 1.1 suggests that leadership has a direct input relationship to all of the components of the model. What the model does not show is the relationship between leadership and the organization's environment, including the agency's funding sources, regulatory bodies, legal system, divergent constituency groups, and, of utmost importance, its clients. According to Lewis, Lewis, and Souflee (1991, pp. 291–292):

> Managerial leaders in the human services must do more than . . . develop technical proficiency in the functions of the managerial process, develop effective leadership skills, and attend to the culture of . . . the organization. Today's managerial leaders must also acquire knowledge and skills in dealing with the . . . organization's environment.

They continue:

> Knowledge of the environments in which human service organizations are embedded and of the skills required to negotiate balanced exchanges of tangible and intangible goods and services between the organization and its task environment becomes an essential component of the managerial leader's professional armamentarium.

The third assumption undergirding the Human Services Management Model—that only under ideal circumstances does one find both managerial and leadership qualities in the same person—implies the obvious: we live in a less than perfect world and our human service organizations (most, at any rate) are less than ideal. Yet, it is exactly the achievement of the ideal that drives organizations obsessed with providing the best possible services to their clients. Furthermore, to be magnificently obsessed by the absolute necessity of providing quality services to clients is but another attribute of a good leader.

Strategic and Tactical Planning

Human service organizations exist for the purpose of meeting the health, welfare, and educational needs of people. The particular purpose of any human service agency is usually contained in its mission statement. In the case of public agencies, their mission is usually found in the piece of legislation that created them. The mission of the private nonprofit agency is determined by its dominant coalition, i.e., its Board of Directors, and reflects the board members' values, perceptions, and commitments.

Mission statements are commonly stated in broad, general terms, such as:

- The purpose of this organization is to meet the economic needs of the indigent citizens of the county who are ineligible for state or federal assistance.
- This agency is established in order to provide counseling and education to individuals and families in matters pertaining to drug abuse.
- The mission of this agency is to enhance the quality of life of the physically handicapped residents of this community.

Any planning done by an organization should be inextricably connected to its mission, if that mission is to be fulfilled. Moreover, planning determines the form and content of the rest of the components of the management system, including the design of the structure of the organization, its staffing pattern, its finances, its delivery of services, and its program efficiency and effectiveness. Therefore, considerable thought must be given to the specification of a program's goals and objectives. Program goals and objectives, furthermore, should be based on a sound analysis of the needs in the community related to the agency's mission.

Once related community needs are analyzed, it is the responsibility of the dominant coalition to establish long-term and short-term goals to meet those needs. Establishment of long-term goals is usually referred to as strategic planning. Intermediate goals designed to meet long-term goals come under the heading of tactical planning.

Although not as general as the mission statement, goals are usually not specific enough to lend themselves to quantitative measurement. Therefore, goals should be accompanied by behavioral objectives stated in measurable terms. Objectives can be of three kinds (United Way Services, 1978): organizational, activity, or outcome. Organizational objectives refer to the agency's intention to improve its operations; activity objectives refer to expected number of services or activities to be accomplished within a specific period of time; outcome objectives specify the impact of program intervention on client behavior.

Designing Organizational Structure

Once program goals and objectives are specified, the structure of the program can be designed. Goals determine the number and types of functions the program will have. For example, a program can have three goals:

1. To provide crisis hotline services.
2. To provide individual and family counseling.
3. To provide family life education.

These goals suggest three program functions. Whether or not to provide these services within one unit or to create three separate service components will depend on strategic choices made by the dominant coalition. The activity objectives corresponding to each of the goals will assist the dominant coalition in determining the service delivery structure of the program. Activity objectives selected and approved by the Board of Directors help determine the number of volunteers, counselors, and education specialists required to efficiently and effectively meet each goal. Lewis, Lewis, and Souflee (1991, pp. 227–278) distinguish between organizational design and structure as follows:

> Organizational structure is, of course, more than organizational design. An organizational design is best depicted by a table of organization or an organizational chart implying relationships among organizational components. Organizational structure, on the other hand, spells out relationships and addresses such issues as centralization/decentralization, liaison devices, unit groupings and unit size, job specialization, and so on.

An example of an organizational chart based on the goals mentioned above is given in Figure 1.2 below.

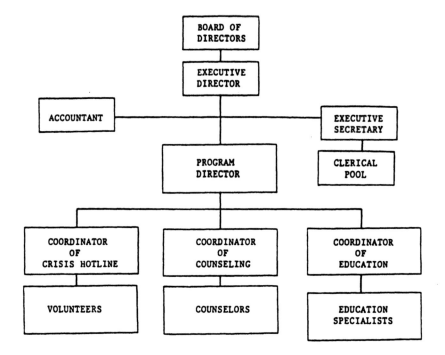

Figure 1.2 Organizational Chart

This chart depicts the basic structure of what Mintzberg (1979) calls the "professional bureaucracy." It consists of a strategic apex, a middle line, and an operating core, support staff and a technostructure. The strategic apex in this example is what we have called the dominant coalition—the Board of Directors and the Executive Director. The middle line is what is often referred to as mid-management. It is comprised of the program director and program coordinators. The operating core consists of the crisis hotline volunteers, the individual and family counselors, and the family life education specialists. These are the workers who apply the functional technologies of the organization to the organization's clients. The support staff include the executive secretary and the clerical pool, with the accountant being the only member of the technostructure, i.e., that part of the organization vital to the organization's operations but outside of the chain of command.

Design and structure issues addressed by this component of the management model include differentiation and integration, centralization and decentralization, chain of command, and span of control. In the above example, differentiation resulted in the creation of three functional components: crisis hotline, counseling, and education. Integration was achieved by placing these components under the oversight of a Program Director, or integrator. Attention to these issues is important as differentiation and integration can be a serious source of intra-organizational conflict—in the absence of an effective integrator—due to the differing orientations, training, and values possessed by staff performing different functions in an organization (Lawrence & Lorsch, 1967). This is especially true in the presence of such factors as intercomponent task interdependencies, status inconsistencies, jurisdictional ambiguities, dependencies on common resources, and so forth (Miles, 1979).

The chain of command in a professional bureaucracy pertains to the line of authority descending from the top to bottom, from the formulation of policy to its implementation. An issue that arises in human service agencies is how much autonomy to grant to the members of the operating core in the execution of their professional duties. In other words, how much centralization or decentralization of power should exist in a human service organization? This question speaks to the values of the dominant coalition and to the leadership styles of its managerial staff.

Span of control refers to the number of supervisees that a manager can effectively and efficiently supervise. One commonly held "rule of thumb" is that a supervisor should not attempt to oversee more than six persons at any given time. Today, however, most theoreticians discount this rule in favor of the examination of contingency factors, such as unit function, staff proficiency, environmental conditions, etc.

Regardless of interpretation, span of control has significance, in part, for the shape of the organization which evolves through growth. Wide span yields a flat structure; short span results in a tall structure. Further, the span concept directs attention to the complexity of human and functional interrelationships in an organization (Scott, 1978, p. 276).

Organizational structure is closely correlated to organizational effectiveness (Mintzberg, 1979). Therefore, it is incumbent upon dominant coalitions of human service enterprises to design structures compatible with agency mission, goals, and objectives.

Establishing Technological Rationality

This element of the human service management model concerns the selection of the relevant technology needed to accomplish organizational goals and objectives within the context of the agency's organizational structure. Achieving technological rationality is measured by the extent to which selected technologies produce desired outcomes. The concept of technological, or technical, rationality originated with Thompson (1967), who also identified three general technologies: the long-linked, the mediating, and the intensive. The long-linked technology is the kind found in mass production assembly lines; the mediating involves using standardized ways to link people, such as telephone customers, together. Human service organizations are especially concerned with the third technology, although they often also employ mediating technologies.

The third technology, the intensive, signifies that a variety of techniques is drawn upon in order to achieve a change in some specific object; but the selection, combination, and order of application are determined by feedback from the object itself. When the object is human, this technology is regarded as "therapeutic" . . . (Thompson, 1967, p. 17).

The degree to which members of the human services "possess" the relevant technologies, coupled with the developmental state of the technologies, will determine, in large measure, the degree of service effectiveness enjoyed by human service organization (Miringoff, 1980). Mediating technologies employed by agencies— that is, technologies such as information and referral, transportation, case management, and the like—are relatively routine and therefore highly developed and not difficult to possess. Intensive technologies, on the other hand, require extensive training in institutions of higher learning charged with the responsibility to develop the state of their respective technologies and to turn out graduates with a high degree of possession of the technologies taught. Human service organizations expect, for example, that an applicant with a Master of Social Work degree will possess a certain level of standardized knowledge and skills, and that that level is higher than the level possessed by an applicant with a Bachelor of Social Work degree. The question before managers responsible for the staffing of the organization becomes one of whether a certain job requires a BSW or an MSW level of technological proficiency.

Not only must direct service staff possess an appropriate level of relevant technology, they must also maintain and evolve knowledge and skills in order to keep pace with technological developments. Service effectiveness therefore requires hat the organization provide structured staff development programs to its workforce in order to achieve and maintain a state-of-the-art service delivery capability.

Additionally, managers of human service agencies must also address the issues of the relevancy of their intensive technologies to the diverse cultural needs of their client populations, and of the degree to which service providers and clients share a common language and world view. No matter how highly developed and possessed the technology, if the practitioner and client are worlds apart culturally, the application of that technology will not have the desired outcomes (Souflee, 1977; Torrey, 1972; Wright, Saleebey, Watts, & Lecca, 1983).

Resource Procurement and Allocation

This component of the management model has to do with the procurement of funds to support the structure and staffing pattern dictated by the agency's planning goals and objectives. Moreover, it has to do as well with the budgeting, or internal allocation, of those funds to support the program activities designed to meet organizational goals and objectives.

Included in this component are the various fund-raising strategies used by staffs and boards of directors to secure financial resources from the environment to maintain and develop program operations. One common strategy employed by private nonprofit organizations is to affiliate with the local United Way to ensure a regular and somewhat predictable source of continual funding. Before engaging in binding affiliative relationships with federations such as United Way, dominant coalitions have to consider and weigh the nonmonetary costs involved. Although affiliated or member agencies maintain their legal autonomy, they may in many instances lose some of their decision-making and functional autonomy, since the trade-off for membership usually means conforming to fiscal and programmatic conditions attached to funding. This is not to say that other funding sources—e.g., federal and state agencies, foundations, etc.—don't attach conditions; most do. It is to say, however, that dominant coalitions must consider the conditions in the light of the coalition's obligation to maintain organizational integrity.

Managers of human service organizations, especially the private nonprofit type, spend a considerable amount of time attending to the financial matters of the organization, including the writing of grants and contracts to attract operating and capital improvement funds. Moreover, it is common for boards of directors to devote a good portion of their attention to fundraising and to the oversight of agency expenditures, since both resource procurement and financial management are duties shared by the board and staff.

Developing the agency's annual budget is usually the responsibility of the executive director. However, this responsibility can be shared with other staff members. Ultimately, though, it is the dominant coalition's responsibility to approve the budget (Mayers, 1989). Sound budget decisions are those which are connected to the achievement of program goals and objectives. Therefore, it is incumbent upon the dominant coalition to make fiscal decisions within that context.

Whereas funding sources used to approve allocations based on incremental budget presentations, this is now rarely the case. That is, agencies can no longer expect that only annual increments to existing budgets must be justified. In this age of zero-based budgeting, agencies must defend and justify their entire budget each funding cycle, and must plan for such contingencies as budget reduction, modest budget increases, or same-level funding (a form of budget reduction, considering inflation). Moreover, agencies with multiple functions or programs are increasingly expected to submit budget requests that clearly specify the amount of resources being allocated to each function or program (Skidmore, 1983; Mayers, 1989).

Two current issues pertaining to the financing of the human service organization have to do with insurance payments and marketing, both of which raise ethical questions. The first, insurance payments, concerns the ethics of terminating services upon the expiration of coverage rather than upon the achievement of treatment goals. The second has to do with the requirement that clinicians generate a certain number of referrals from the community in order to retain their jobs.

Resource procurement and allocation require both technical and sociopolitical knowledge and skills on the part of the dominant coalition, the managers, and the staff of the human service enterprise. Questions of ethics and equity must be resolved in order to avoid conflicts resulting from the management of the financial affairs of the organization.

Coordination and Control

The coordination and control of agency or program operations is a major managerial function consisting of several sub-elements, including the provision of leadership; the establishment of agency policies and procedures; devising ways of collecting, using, and disseminating information; managing intra-organizational conflict; and the establishment of relationships with the agency's task environment. Coordination, according to Mintzberg (1979) is "the glue that holds organizations together" (p. 3). Control, on the other hand, refers to regulated flows of information and decision making (e.g., commands, policies) vertically and horizontally within the organization.

Although an organization can have more than one "power center" (Etzioni, 1964), and leadership responsibilities can be assigned to various individuals at different levels of the organizational hierarchy, principal leadership functions for most human service organizations are usually officially lodged at the highest level of the organization, the Board of Directors and the Chief Executive Officer—that part of the organization that Chandler (1962) calls the "dominant coalition" and that Mintzberg (1979) refers to as the "strategic apex."

The coordinating function of the Board of Directors is usually confined to external agency relations, such as fundraising and networking, and its control function is usually delimited to the formulation of policy and the review and monitoring of policy implementation. The Chief Executive Officer, while also heavily charged with environmental relations, such as fundraising, the development of interagency agreements, public relations, and similar external coordinating activities, is held primarily accountable for the establishment and implementation of internal coordinating and control mechanisms, including the management of intra-organizational conflict that results from coordination and control efforts.

Coordination and control are two sides of the same coin. Coordination of activities is less likely to occur in the absence of a strong power center. The authority vested in the dominant coalition either by laws or constitutions (i.e., bylaws) that sanction human service organizations, give those coalitions the power to control program operations. Without that control, coordination is an improbable goal. Yet, control should not necessarily connote centralized, authoritarian bureaucracy, although in the absence of democratic, participatory leadership, it can have exactly that result. Nevertheless, participative and laissez-faire leadership are not synonymous. The latter can be as deleterious as the totalitarian style.

Control should be based on strategic decisions made at the top as informed by feedback originating at the bottom of the organization. Mintzberg (1979, pp. 42–43) refers to this process as "regulated control flows," i.e., commands and instructions are fed down the chain of authority, emanating from the strategic apex . . . and elaborated as they flow downward. In the formal planning process, for example, general "strategic" plans are established at the strategic apex; successively, these are elaborated into programs, capital and operating budgets, and operating plans . . . finally reaching the operating core as sets of detailed work instructions. In effect, in the regulated system the decisions made at the strategic apex set off ever-widening waves of implementational decisions as they flow down the hierarchy. Mintzberg continues:

> The upward control system exists as a "management information system," or MIS, that collects and codes data on performance, starting in the operating core. As this information passes each level in the hierarchy, it is aggregated until, finally, it reaches the strategic apex as a broad summary of overall organizational performance. (p. 43)

Program Implementation

Once funds are secured based on an approved budget, program operations can begin. The executive director can now turn his or her attention to the hiring of the program director, who, in turn, will be responsible for the hiring of staff in accordance with predetermined decisions regarding the establishment and achievement of technological rationality.

It is at this point that the decisions made with regard to coordination and control mechanisms come into full play. One useful tool in implementing programs is the time line. This device specifies which task is to be accomplished by what time and by whom. The time line assists in keeping program operations on course. Coordination and control mechanisms also include the collection, analysis, and use of data and information regarding service delivery, financial transactions, interagency agreements, policy and procedural decisions, staff performance, etc. Establishing the program's infrastructure—i.e., securing office space, purchasing of equipment and supplies, setting up a communication system, etc.—are some of the initial concerns of the program director. Once staff are on board, attention must be paid to their orientation to the program and to their specific responsibilities.

In most human service agencies, front line supervisors play a key role in program implementation, in assuring that organizational mission, goals, and objectives are met. Supervisors are at the nexus between the two major technologies—administration and direct practice—of the organization. Where the two technologies meet, service goals are operationalized into service activities. It is the responsibility of the supervisor to articulate the two technologies in a manner which satisfies the requirements of each in the efficient and effective implementation of services. The supervisor serves as the link between policy formulation and policy implementation (Lewis, Lewis, & Souflee, 1991). According to Williams:

> Implementation in an organization can involve both a continuing effort over time to raise the capability of that organization . . . to carry out programs or projects, and a one time effort to put an organizational decision into place. (1976, p. 3)

The human service supervisor is concerned with both types of implementation.

Exciting as it is to implement new programs, the challenges are formidable. As Hasenfeld (1987, p. 463) observes:

> The period of initial implementation of program technology is a period of trial and error. It requires a great deal of flexibility and no little tolerance for failure and for ambiguity. Open-mindedness and willingness to explore alternative routes are essential ingredients. During the early stages of program development, lines of communication with staff and clients must be kept as open as possible. Feedback is essential if the program is to adjust to unexpected exigencies. Staff who work directly with the community can provide invaluable information on the operationalization of the technology and its problems, its failures, and its successes.

Another important dimension of program implementation pertains to the external relationships that the organization forms with key stakeholders in its task environment. Primary among these are the program's client population. Without clients, there is no program. Therefore, efforts must be made to inform the populace about the services of the agency and to enlist the help of established agencies in referring clients. The formulation of clear and easily understood eligibility requirements is essential from the start.

Inadequate interpretation of an agency's services or intake

policy may result in inappropiate referrals. An agency that turns away many ineligible clients causes a serious and unnecessary hardship to those clients and to its staff as well. It also does harm to its own image, often damaging its relationships to other agencies. Thus it is critical for the new program to disseminate accurate and specific information about eligibility, both to the public and to other social agencies (Hasenfeld, 1987, p. 465).

In addition to establishing agreements with other agencies for the purpose of their referring clients to the organization, it is necessary as well to develop means by which the organization's clients can be referred for supplementary services to other community agencies. This sort of reciprocity between the organization and the human services community is essential in fostering organizational visibility and credibility.

Program Evaluation

The final component of the human services management model is program evaluation. Program evaluation has its origins in strategic and tactical planning, at the point where program goals and objectives are specified. In fact, program evaluation designs are structured around the types of objectives contained in program goals. For example, activities objectives dictate the use of efficiency evaluation measurements, whereas outcome objectives call for effectiveness evaluation designs. Thus, evaluation findings serve to inform the agency's dominant coalition of whether or not program goals and objectives are being or have been met efficiently and effectively. Based on findings, the dominant coalition is informed to make decisions around several issues pertaining to program operations:

> Information about current activities can help decision makers deal with immediate issues concerning resource allocations, staffing patterns, and provision of services to individual clients or target populations. At the same time, data concerning the outcomes of services can lead the way toward more rational decisions about continuation or expansion of effective programs and contraction or elimination of less effective services. Decisions concerning the development of new programs or the selection of alternate forms of service can also be made, not necessarily on the basis of evaluation alone but with evaluative data making a significant contribution. (Lewis, Lewis, & Souflee, 1991, p. 234)

In this age of social services accountability, the trend is for funding sources to demand not only efficiency evaluations related to cost-per-unit of services delivered, but also outcome evaluations which measure the impact of services on the lives of clients. The latter demand the use of one or more evaluation designs ranging from highly sophisticated to rather primitive means of determining the effects of intervention on human behavior. Whichever design is used turns on the agency's consideration of the ethical, practical, and economic issues peculiar to each design. The more sophisticated approaches to program evaluation attempt to establish a cause-effect relationship between intervention and behavior. The least sophisticated approaches tap clients' level of satisfaction with services rendered. In between, there are designs that measure individuals' behavioral changes during service delivery, and those that measure changes in attitudes and feelings. Although these approaches make no claims about cause-effect relationships, they can produce qualified correlations between treatment and outcomes. In selecting the evaluation designs to measure program outcomes, the dominant coalition and its funding source need to consider the practical, affordable, and ethical ramifications of each approach.

Program evaluation can occur during and after the implementation of a program. Evaluations which take place during program operations are called formative, process, or effort evaluations. Those performed at the end of a specific period of program operations are called summative (Weiss, 1972). Human services managers concerned with the provision of quality services need to consider incorporating both formative and summative evaluation procedures into their program implementation plans.

Finally, both the funding source and the focal organization have to realize that program evaluation, although touted as a rational process, is fraught with political implications—evaluation is a rational enterprise that takes place in a political context. Political considerations intrude in three major ways, and the evaluator who fails to recognize their presence is in for a series of shocks and frustrations. First, the policies and programs with which evaluations deal are the creatures of political decisions. They were proposed, defined, debated, enacted, and funded through political processes; and in implementation they remain subject to pressures, both supportive and hostile, which arise out of the play of politics. Second, because evaluation is undertaken in order to feed into decision making, its reports enter the political arena. There, evaluative evidence of program outcomes has to compete for attention with other factors that carry weight in the political process. Third, and perhaps least recognized, evaluation itself is a political stance. By its very nature, it makes implicit political statements about such issues as the problematic nature of some programs and the unassailableness of others, the legitimacy of program goals, the legitimacy of program strategies, the utility of strategies of incremental reform, and even the appropriate role of the social scientist in policy and program formation (Weiss, 1975, pp. 13–14).

Conclusion
ھ

Program evaluation completes the cycle of the human services management model, which, as a systemic and dynamic process, lends itself to iterative and heuristic opportunities for the improvement of program operations. But, as Hasenfeld (1987) has observed, the initial steps are critical in the quest for program efficiency and effectiveness. Through repetition and self-discovery, managers of human service organizations can detect the pitfalls and learn the ropes of operating successful programs based on optimal decisions regarding each of the elements of the model.

Case illustrations in this text bring into bas-relief the everyday but critical dynamics of organizational behavior as they pertain to the components of the management model. These cases serve to depict the humor, the pathos, the rational, the irrational, the mundane, and the other myriad dimensions of life in the human service organization.

References

Abels, P., & Murphy, M. J. (1981). *Administration in the human services: A normative systems approach.* Englewood Cliffs, NJ: Prentice-Hall.

Barnard, C. I. (1968). *The functions of the executive.* Cambridge, MA: Harvard University Press.

Chandler, A. (1962). *Strategy and structure: Chapters in the history of the industrial enterprise.* Cambridge, MA: The MIT Press.

Etzioni, A. (1964). *Modern organizations.* Englewood Cliffs, NJ: Prentice-Hall.

Evans, M. G. (1979). Leadership. In S. Kerr (Ed.), *Organizational behavior* (pp. 207–239). Columbus, Ohio: Grid Publishing.

Hasenfeld, Y. (1987). Program development. In F. M. Cox, J. L. Erlich, J. Rothman, & J. E. Tropman (Eds.), *Strategies of community organization*, 4th Ed., (pp. 450–473). Itasca, IL: F. E. Peacock.

Lawrence, P. R., & Lorsch, J. (1967). *Organization and behavior.* Cambridge, MA: Harvard University Press.

Lewis, J. A., Lewis, M. D., & Souflee, F. (1991). *Management of human service programs.* Pacific Grove, CA: Brooks/Cole.

Mayers, R. S. (1989). *Financial management for nonprofit human service agencies.* Springfield, IL: Charles C Thomas.

Miles, R. H. (1979). *Macro organizational behavior.* Santa Monica, CA: Goodyear Publishing.

Mintzberg, H. (1979). *The structuring of organizations.* Englewood Cliffs, NJ: Prentice-Hall.

Miringoff, M. L. (1980). *Management in human service organizations.* New York: Macmillan.

Patti, R. J. (1983). *Social welfare administration: Managing social programs in a developmental context.* Englewood Cliffs, NJ: Prentice-Hall.

Perlmutter, F. D. & Slavin, S. (Eds.) (1980). *Leadership in social administration: Perspectives for the 1980's.* Philadelphia, PA: Temple University Press.

Scott, W. G. (1978). Organizational theory: An overview and an appraisal. In J. M. Shafritz and P. H. Whitbeck (Eds.), *Classics of organization and theory* (pp. 274–290). Oak Park, IL: Moore.

Selznick, P. (1957). *Leadership in administration: A sociological interpretation.* New York: Harper & Row.

Skidmore, R. A. (1983). *Social work administration: Dynamic management of human relations.* Englewood Cliffs, NJ: Prentice-Hall.

Souflee, F. (1977). Social work: The acquiescing profession. *Social Work, 22*(5), 419–421.

Thompson, J. D. (1967). *Organizations in action.* New York: McGraw-Hill.

Torrey, E. F. (1972). *The mind game: Witchdoctors and psychiatrists.* New York: Bantam Books.

United Way Services (1978). *Program planning and performance measurement system.* Cleveland, Ohio: United Way Services.

Weiss, C. H. (1972). *Evaluation research: Methods of assessing program effectiveness.* Englewood Cliffs, NJ: Prentice-Hall.

Weiss, C. H. (1975). Evaluation research in the political context. In E. L. Struening & M. Guttentag (Eds.), *Handbook of evaluation research*, Vol. 1. (pp. 13–26). Beverly Hills, CA: Sage Publications.

Wright, R., Saleebey, D., Watts, T. D., & Lecca, P. (1983). *Transcultural perspectives in the human services: Organizational issues and trends.* Springfield, IL: Charles C. Thomas.

è∆ Chapter Two

The Case Method

THE CASE METHOD APPROACH

The case method is a type of teaching in which case studies become "pedagogical tools to bring problems and approaches from the managerial world to the classroom" (Bocker, 1987, p. 64). The case method approach to education and training dates back to the Socratic technique of teaching people to think as opposed to just memorizing facts and theories (Kelly, 1983). This approach has many advantages over traditional classroom lecturing as it uses a systematic system for developing and enhancing analytical and problem-solving skills. In this approach, students are more likely to remember concepts and theories when they can apply them to real life problems and issues (Andrews & Noel, 1986). This is an active, as opposed to a passive, approach to learning. In active learning, attempts at problem solving become deeply embedded in memory and are thus available for retrieval at a later date (Spizizen & Hart, 1985). In fact, the case method stimulates learning more than lecture teaching (Bocker, 1987).

Two types of cases used in the case method are the demonstration case and the problem case (Bocker, 1987). The demonstration case shows effective management style or decision making by demonstrating how a manager or supervisor acted in a given situation. The problem case enables the student to identify, analyze, and solve a specific management problem on his/her own rather than be given a solution. The guidelines for case analysis used in this book ask the student to place himself or herself in the role of the manager and develop appropriate alternative solutions to a problem.

A good case study should also enable the student to form his/her own resolution or moral/ethical judgement regarding the issue(s) of the case. It should be open and flexible enough to lead the student through certain analytic processes including: the factual issues, the normative issues, the available alternatives and an appropriate defendable decision (Gini, 1985).

While some have criticized the case method approach as being too rigid and repressing creative thinking (Argyris, 1980), our experience has been the opposite. Students can learn important lessons by analyzing cases and discussing them with classmates. One principle they learn is that there are not always correct answers to difficult management problems, just alternative ways of dealing with them. Discussions in the classroom often turn into brainstorming sessions which generate previously unthought of solutions. The second principle they learn is that any decision they make, while often based on unstated assumptions, should lend itself to articulation in a rationale manner with logic and data.

GUIDELINES FOR USING THE CASE METHOD

Table 2.1 illustrates a framework and guidelines for students to follow in reading and using the cases. The guidelines help the student walk through the decision-making process, forcing them to look at factors and alternatives and develop logical rationales for their decisions.

Each case provides an overview of the setting in which the action occurs, a profile of the key actors involved, and other information needed by the student to make decisions and demonstrate mastery of a given concept. At the end of each case, the assumption is that the student is the administrator who must make critical decisions regarding the issues involved. The student can use the guidelines given here as the basis for a paper, presentation, or discussion.

The framework presented here is a *suggested* approch that we have found very useful with our administration and planning students. However, it is only a suggestion for instructors. A professor is free to use another model that s/he is more comfortable with, or to have students address particular aspects of a case by asking the questions found at the end of each case.

Table 2.1 Guidelines for Analyzing a Management Case

In reading these management cases for analysis and discussion, please review the following areas:

1. **Facts of the Case:**
   What events transpired that have a bearing on this case? Who are the principal actors involved?
2. **Issues:**
   What are the broad issues involved in this case? How do opposing sides view the issues, e.g., management vs. staff? What are problems in value arena and professional ethical standards?
3. **Alternative Actions:**
   What alternative actions could be taken in this case? Please list all the possibilities that you can think of. Do not rule out any at this point. You should be able to list many more than simple extremes. What are the possible scenarios that may be addressed in this problematic situation on the continuum from disasterious approach to a reasonable competent approach to the most ideal or ethical professional approach? Also, add what are implications for professional practice within the NASW Code of Ethics?
4. **Recommendations:**
   Out of all the alternative actions you listed, choose at least one to recommend.
   A. What action(s) have you chosen and why?
   B. What are the advantages and disadvantages of the action(s) you have chosen? How do they outweigh the other alternatives that you had to chose from?
   C. How feasible are your recommendations and what political considerations must be taken into account to make them work?
   D. What assumptions did you use in coming to your decision on these recommendations?
5. **Self-Awareness of Principles for Management Practice:**
   What have you learned from this case that can benefit you as a manager? What experiences have you had that come to mind when reading this case, and what have you learned from those experiences that helps you here?

Human service managers are responsible to governing boards or to their supervisors, to funding sources, and to regulatory bodies that desire and demand logical, rational, well thought out reasons for a course of action. If an administrative/planning student develops the ability to recognize and choose from alternative courses of action by use of this book, s/he will become a more credible, authoritative leader. All good managers use intuitive, "gut" feelings of course, but such insights come from cues triggered by experience. The student or manager should be able to utilize these nonverbal cues in the development of a strategic, well reasoned approach. This is the basis for the framework presented.

Nevertheless, we are not under any illusions that as managers or as human beings we are ever completely rational in our decision making. We can never gather enough information or be able to fully evaluate the data we receive. But managers must: a) be cognizant of the fundamental principles underlying significant decisions reached; and b) be capable of articulating them convincingly to significant others within and without the organization. We trust that the use of these cases will help build such capacity among students while offering them a glimpse of those varied dilemmas encountered daily by practitioners in the field.

References

Andrews, E. S., & Noel, J. L. (1986). Adding life to the case-study method. *Training and Development Journal, 40*(2), 28–29.

Argyris, C. (1980). Some limitations of the case method: Experiences in a management development program. *Academy of Management Review, 5*(2), 291–298.

Bocker, F. (1987). Is case teaching more effective than lecture teaching in business administration? An exploratory analysis. *Interfaces, 17*(5), 64–71.

Gini, A. R. (1985). The case method: A perspective. *Journal of Business Ethics, 4*(4), 351–352.

Kelly, H. (1983). Case method training: What it is, how it works. *Training, 20*(2), 46–49.

Spizizen, G., & Hart, C.W.L. (1985). Active learning and the case method: Theory and practice. *Cornell Hotel & Restaurant Administration Quarterly (CHR), 26*(2), 63–66.

Cases

CASE ONE

ꝥ

An Accounting Clerk for DSS

The State Department of Social Services (DSS) has a centralized
accounting system in which all expenditures by branch units (called
Areas) are processed at headquarters. Area Directors are authorized
to approve purchases up to $1,000 within an established annual
budget. The Area units do not disburse payments against any expenses incurred, and are dependent on the Central office for a
monthly accounting of expenditures by the Area unit. The problem
is that Central is so slow it takes them months to send the expense
sheets to the units. It would be easy for a unit to incur a deficit without someone to keep a daily record of the invoices, vouchers, and
purchase orders that are processed and sent to Central.

Bonnie McCarthy had been a secretary who was asked to keep
track of expenditures by the Area unit. She did the best she could,
but she really had no knowledge of bookkeeping or accounting. She
devised a simple ledger system to keep track of the books, but she
was constantly behind in her entries. So she was transferred back
to secretarial duties, and the position of accounting clerk was created to attract a more qualified person.

As the Department of Social Services is a unit of state government, there are civil service regulations as well as union rules about
hiring. One of the rules is that vacant positions have to be adver-
tised internally before someone from outside can be sought. In addition, employees of the department have preference for a job over an
outsider. This sometimes means that departments that are trying
to "get rid of" unsatisfactory employees can dump them on another

unwitting department. It was difficult to know when and if this is being done in any particular case. An astute Area Director has to ask around informally, because no matter how bad the employee, he/she always comes with glowing references.

Maggie Carter was hired as an accounting clerk for the Area unit run by Roland Sipes. She had transferred in from the central accounting department at headquarters where she worked for a number of years. The Area Director was very happy to get someone he thought was so qualified. He had been told that she was quite familiar with the procedures for processing purchase orders and vouchers, as well as taking care of grants monies. She was to be supervised by the clerical supervisor of the department, Yolanda Green.

Yolanda Green supervised all the nonprofessional staff of the office and had done so for a number of years. Roland Sipes was new to the position of Area Director, having been with the DSS for a little over a year. Previously he had been the Executive Director of a small nonprofit agency. Roland and Yolanda worked well together, she functioned as his assistant and oversaw the day-to-day operations of the office. One of Roland's and Yolanda's problems, however, was that he thought he could run the Area office the way he had run his nonprofit agency. She took it upon herself to constantly run interference for him and smooth things over with other departments. He seemed to not understand, nor care about, civil service or union procedures and contracts. This led to the predicament that involved Maggie Carter.

Maggie Carter had received glowing references from her former supervisors, she assured Yolanda that she understood the Department procedures for processing all the financial forms and paperwork. Soon after she started her new job in the unit, however, it became apparent to Yolanda Green that Maggie could not do the job. Yolanda decided to give Maggie time to adjust. She also sent her to numerous in-service trainings provided by the Department for staff involved in the accounting procedures. Nevertheless, Yolanda had to help Maggie perform some of the functions of her job, because she always seemed so swamped in trying to do her bookkeeping and forms processing. This caused Yolanda to fall behind on her own work. She mentioned to the Director that Maggie was slow in learning the job, but nothing was ever said to Maggie herself.

Yolanda gradually learned that Maggie had a number of personal problems that interfered with her ability to concentrate on her job. These involved her husband and grown children who still lived at home with her. Because civil service employees could accumulate unused sick leave indefinitely, Maggie began taking sick days off to attend to her family problems. Maggie got further and further behind at work. It now took weeks for a simple purchase order to be processed. Yolanda became more angry and frustrated at Maggie's inability to do her job and at having to do some of it herself. After months of this, Yolanda called Maggie in and gave her a verbal warning regarding her performance. She also suggested specific ways that she could improve her work habits.

Maggie's primary responsibility was to be able to tell the Director how much money remained in the Area budget at a moment's notice. She was also supposed to be able to tell him how much had been spent in any budget category. Because she was so far behind in her work, she was unable to do this.

One day about three months before the end of the fiscal year, the Director received a call from Headquarters telling him that the Area expense account was overdrawn by $7,000. This meant that his unit had a deficit and would have to charge expenses for the rest of the fiscal year to the following year's budget. The Director became enraged and announced at the next day's professional staff meeting that he was going to fire Maggie. He told the group that she was incompetent and responsible for the deficit.

Meanwhile, Yolanda gave Maggie a written warning regarding her performance, detailing a number of areas that had been less than satisfactory. Maggie angrily wrote a response denying all the allegations. In her response, Maggie pointed out that she had worked at that particular unit of the Agency for almost a year and had never received any feedback, positive or negative, about her work. She asked if her work had been so bad, why had no one said anything to her before?

That same week, on a day that Yolanda was out of the office, Roland Sipes called Maggie into his office. Maggie assumed he wanted to talk with her regarding her performance; she had heard from some of the social workers about his comments in the staff meeting.

When she walked into his office, Roland started yelling at Maggie, accusing her of incompetence. She tried to explain to him her version of what had happened, but he wouldn't listen. He told her he didn't want to hear anything she had to say, all he wanted was her resignation. She told him she was trying to transfer to another branch, but he exclaimed that she was so incompetent no other branch wanted her. She said she would try harder to do a better job. He yelled that he was going to document everything she did until he had enough to fire her. All the clerical pool staff in the outer office could hear the yelling emanating from behind Roland's door and became very angry at Roland for his treatment of Maggie.

Shaken and crying, Maggie left Roland's office and called the union. Upon her return, Yolanda was contacted by the union person representing Maggie. Maggie had filed a grievance against the Department. Since Yolanda was her supervisor, she had to respond in Step One of the grievance process. When she was informed of what had transpired between Roland and Maggie, Yolanda realized there was no way that Maggie could now be fired. She also knew that she could not let the grievance go to Step Two, which would involve Roland. As his assistant, she had acquired more status and control over agency operations. She knew that he did not have the self-discipline to deal calmly with confrontations. If Roland yelled at Maggie or said derogatory things about her in front of the union rep, it would make the agency's case worse no matter what Maggie's performance level was. Roland had violated strict union and civil service procedures for disciplining and terminating an employee (see Appendix I for a brief synopsis of the procedures).

Questions
ಇ

1. Has Maggie properly utilized remedies available to state employees under established personnel policies and the union contract?

2. What would you do now if you were Yolanda?

3. What should Roland do now? What should he have done before?

APPENDIX I:
EXCERPTS FROM THE AGENCY PERSONNEL MANUAL

Section V: Performance Evaluations

Each department is encouraged to develop a method for evaluating all personnel after six months of employment and annually thereafter. The method devised must be uniform for all employees, and must be communicated to all employees. Employees must receive a copy of their performance evaluations and a copy must be placed in their personnel files.

Section VI: Termination Procedures

Employees whose performance is below standard must be given an opportunity to improve said performance. Employees must be given notice in writing as to those areas of substandard work, a time frame as to when improvement is expected, and consequences of unchanged productivity. During this period, employee will also be notified as to when and how often reviews of work will take place.

APPENDIX II:
EXCERPTS FROM THE UNION CONTRACT BINDING THE DEPARTMENT OF SOCIAL SERVICES AND THE STATE EMPLOYEES UNION.

Article 8: Grievance Procedures

1. Any grievance by an employee shall be handled in the following manner:

   Step 1: The grievance shall be presented within ten (10) working days after the occurrence of the event. The grievance shall be presented in writing citing the alleged violation. The grievance shall normally be presented to the employee's immediate supervisor. If the employee so requests, the steward may be present at any meeting that takes place.

   Step 2: If the grievance is not resolved at Step 1, the employee or the Union may within five (5) working days forward the grievance to the second level of authority.* This second level of authority shall within ten (10) working days hold a meeting. The second level of authority shall send his/

---

*The second level of authority refers to the next highest level supervisor in the chain of command. The same applies to the third level.

her written answer within five (5) working days of such meeting.

Step 3: If the Union is not satisfied with the Step 2 answer, the Union may within three (3) working days of receipt of that answer submit to the Office of Personnel a written request for a Third Step Hearing. Such hearing shall take place not later than five (5) working days after receipt of the written request. The employee shall be entitled to be present. The steward, and/or the Union President or his/her designee shall be present.

The Third Step Hearing Officer shall have his/her written decision to the employee and to the Union within five (5) working days after such hearing.

Step 4: If the Union is not satisfied with the decision of the Third Step Hearing Officer, the Union may within ten (10) working days after the receipt of the written decision submit the grievance to binding arbitration.

The Agency and the Union agree that the arbitrator to be chosen jointly shall be selected from a panel or panels to be provided by the American Arbitration Association.

2. The Agency shall provide a copy of any written reprimand to an employee and at his/her request to the steward. The employee shall sign such reprimand, the signature serving only to acknowledge that he/she has read the reprimand. Any employee may file a grievance with respect to any document written to the employee which expresses dissatisfaction with his/her work performance or conduct and with which he/she does not agree.

When an employee's record is free from any disciplinary action for a period of one year, any letters of reprimand or documents which express dissatisfaction with the employee's work performance or conduct in the employee's record shall be removed.

CASE TWO

❧
Status Quo Leadership

Nine months after applying for the position of policy analyst with the state Department of Human Resources, Barbara was called in for an interview with the Commissioner of the department, Mr. Winterman. She had already been interviewed by the Deputy Commissioner, Mr. Morton, several months before, and had not expected to hear from the department again. She was still interested in the position, however, so she agreed to fly to the state capital to be interviewed by Mr. Winterman. Before leaving, she told her boss at the City Planning Department that she might just possibly be offered the job by the state.

Barbara had learned of the opening for the position of policy analyst from a friend who worked as legislative liaison in the Governor's Office. In fact, the position had been created at the request of the Governor, who strongly felt that each state department should critically analyze its policies on a continuous basis to determine if they were having their intended effect. The request, her friend informed her, had only reluctantly been honored by Commissioner Winterman, who felt that his department's policies were beyond reproach.

The position, as Barbara understood it from the job announcement mailed to her by her friend, called for someone with a Master's degree in either public administration or social work, with at least five years' experience in program planning and policy analysis. Duties of the position included the analysis of the department's policies, their formulation and implementation, as well as their effect on clients. The policy analyst served in a consultant capacity to the department's regional administrators in the implementation of departmental policies at the regional and local levels. As someone with an MSW with a concentration in planning and policy analysis, and seven years experience as a city planner, Barbara felt qualified for the position. She looked forward with confidence to her interview with Commissioner Winterman.

Barbara's interview with the Commissioner lasted all of fifteen minutes, during which time Mr. Winterman spent most of it citing "war stories" about his role in developing the department from a "horse and buggy" operation into one of the state's largest agencies. He really didn't see a need for a policy analyst, but since the Governor had insisted that he create the position, he had. Now he was offering the position to Barbara. Perhaps as someone new to the department, she would be able to identify policy flaws no one else had detected. If she did find flaws, she could count on his 100% support in correcting them. Feeling challenged by his remarks, Barbara accepted the position, whereupon the Commissioner took her to his Executive Secretary to fill out the necessary personnel forms. The secretary instructed Barbara to report to Deputy Commissioner Morton on the first working day of the following month, at 9 A.M.

Barbara arrived at her new job early. She went to Deputy Commissioner Morton's office suite and introduced herself to Marlene, his secretary, who asked her to have a seat until Mr. Morton came in. At 9:15, Marlene informed Barbara that "Mr. M." had just called to say he was tied up in a meeting with the State Finance Committee, and that she, Marlene, was to show Barbara to her office and introduce her to Dee, her secretary. Barbara was shown to a small partitioned office space with a desk, a swivel chair, a telephone, and a side chair. To her dismay, she discovered that Dee was located in the secretarial pool on the floor above, where Barbara went to introduce herself.

Dee quickly informed Barbara that she had been with the department for 20 years and had once been the Commissioner's secretary, but that "office politics" and his jealous wife had resulted in her assignment to the secretarial pool, where she had spent the last 12 years being assigned to "break in" new hires such as Barbara. Barbara was not to worry about a thing. Dee would get her a set of office supplies and copies of the agency's policies and have them on her desk first thing in the morning. Barbara wondered if she could have the policy manuals at once so she could start orienting herself to the agency. Dee said she would try to do that. Upon returning to her office, Barbara called Marlene to find out if Mr. M. could see her later in the day. "Sorry," Marlene had said, but Mr. M. had a full schedule, would be flying to a meeting in Pittsburgh the following morning, and would not be back until Monday. Maybe he could see her then.

Barbara spent the remainder of her first day as policy analyst introducing herself to the few people who were at their desks in her work area. Most were cordial but uncommunicative. Only one, Leo, a lawyer assigned to track federal legislation affecting the department, showed any interest in Barbara or her job. By 3 P.M., she called Dee to ask about the policy manuals. The secretary who answered Dee's phone said Dee had taken the afternoon off to look after a sick friend.

Two weeks after reporting for work, Barbara got her office supplies, a stack of folders containing policy memos, and an appointment with her supervisor, Mr. M., who apologized profusely for having been unavailable until then. He congratulated Barbara on getting the position, said he looked forward to working with her, and informed her that she was scheduled to attend, together with other new state employees, a 2-week training session on Management by Objectives to be held in the Department of Agriculture. This workshop was designed to help new state managers teach their supervisees the MBO system of articulating personal and unit objectives with agency goals and mission. When Barbara reminded Mr. M. that she had no supervisees other than Dee, he said that she would find the training useful anyway. The rest of the meeting with Mr. M. consisted of Barbara's futile attempts to learn exactly what she was expected to do as policy analyst and what authority she had, if any, in effecting policy changes at the state, regional, and local levels.

It was not until she got home that evening that Barbara was able to sort out the double-talk, the evasiveness, the glossing over of Mr. M.'s response to her questions. Number one, she had no authority whatsoever. Her department-level policy recommendations were to be submitted to Mr. M., who would forward them with comments to the Executive Committee of the Department, comprised of all division deputy commissioners, for review and comment. The Executive Committee would then send its review of her recommendations to Commissioner Winterman, who would ultimately decide which parts of the report to present to the Board of the Department of Human Resources for action. As far as regional policies were concerned, Barbara was to serve as a consultant to Regional Administrators. In other words, they would ask for her help when they needed it. Moreover, under no circumstances was she to engage in the examination of local policy implementation without the written authority of Regional Administrators and the request of local program directors.

During the next 4 months, Barbara gathered all of the policy memos in effect and organized them into a policy manual. She prepared a separate document containing her analysis of each policy in terms of its short- and long-term consequences on both the department and its clients. Because of Dee's frequent absences from the office on sick-leave or emergency-leave, it took her a full month to type and correct the two documents, which Barbara finally presented to Deputy Commissioner Morton, who promised he would "get to them at the earliest opportunity."

Having completed the department-level analysis, Barbara turned her attention to the regions. Since she had met the Regional Administrators at a state office meeting, she felt comfortable in calling them for individual conferences in their regional offices to offer her services. Only three of the RAs were able to squeeze her into their busy schedules. Of those three, two canceled their appointments at the last minute. The one RA she met with seriously doubted that his region needed Barbara's help.

Toward the end of her first year with the Department of Human Resources, Barbara's policy manual and analysis report are still being reviewed by Mr. M., no regional office has requested her consultation, and Dee is continuing to take time off to sit with an interminable list of sick friends. Barbara's resignation is to the point: "I quit!" Mr. Morton wishes her success in her future endeavors.

Questions
❧

1. As is the case with most agency planners, Barbara was hired in a staff position outside the line of authority. What strategies could Barbara have used in her position to have her plans considered for implementation?

2. Discuss the pros and cons of the strategy employed by the Governor.

3. Should Barbara have quit or should she have taken other steps to address the department's organizational inertia?

CASE THREE

ভ

Developing an Information System

Bernie considers himself an innovator in his local family service agency. As a counselor, he had always kept informed of new treatment techniques. Last year, he was promoted to his current position of Director of Counseling. He is a popular manager, because he devotes considerable energy to making his department run well.

During his masters level education, Bernie used a personal computer for word processing, tax preparation, and other home chores. He always read computer magazines and enjoyed keeping up with technology developments. Bernie knew that computers could help with agency paperwork and record keeping. When a friend offered Bernie a used computer for the agency, Bernie decided to computerize the client record-keeping system of one of his programs, a federally-funded drug treatment center. He wanted to illustrate the potential of a computerized information system to help manage program records. To avoid the resentment of other employees, Bernie did not let the process of computerizing the drug treatment records interfere with his normal work. Programming was mostly done at home, after hours, and on weekends. He had help from a student intern who used the information system as a class project. The executive director seemed excited about Bernie's efforts and often mentioned his computerization project as something innovative that management was doing to help workers.

Within a year, Bernie had successfully computerized the client records of the drug treatment program. These records were mandated by the federal grant and contained many treatment and success measures. Clerical staff of the drug treatment program entered the data into the computer and reports were automatically produced daily, weekly, and monthly. Everyone liked the timeliness of the reports. The counselors especially liked the capability of having clerical staff produce special reports. A typical request was to list the treatment modality and outcome of all clients who scored similar to their client on an addictions test battery. This information was very helpful in developing realistic treatment goals.

Bernie wanted to apply computer power to the record-keeping system of the general counseling program. This computerization would affect staff throughout the agency, since most agency programs shared a common record format. Nevertheless, Bernie saw that computerizing the manual information system would lock in the existing way of doing things. Current data collection methods and forms would be difficult to change once they were programmed in the computer. In addition, Bernie wanted to use the computer's information processing capabilities to solve some of the problems with the manual system. One of these problems was workload equity. Currently, new clients were assigned to counselors with the least number of cases, unless the counselor conducting the initial interview decided to keep the case. Many counselors, who were not usually on-call during peak admitting times, expressed to Bernie privately that they were overworked. They felt they were assigned the more difficult and chronic cases. Others suggested that they should have fewer cases because they achieved more complex outcomes with their clients. That is, they worked on total personal adjustment rather than eliminating a few symptoms. Another problem was that management was coming under pressure by funding sources to document the cost of services and the results of agency intervention. Such documentation was impossible with the manual system.

Bernie's first task was to find software that fit his needs. He found software that allowed an agency to use problem oriented diagnosis and goal attainment scaling with progress notes. It could also be integrated with an accounting system. The software only cost $3,000. This was a bargain considering the work required for his agency to develop its own information system. For only $10,000, the agency could purchase the computers and software required for this move into the computer age.

Bernie developed a computer demonstration of the proposed system. Counseling records would contain data on all client problems and the extent of change on each problem. With the new client record system in place, client workload issues could be solved. Client problem and change data could be combined with other data to calculate work load. Staff and management would decide what variables to include in the work load system and the weight of each variable. A work load measure could be instantly available for each counselor whenever a new case was assigned. Bernie was excited and knew others would be also. He felt he had prepared everyone by successfully computerizing the drug treatment program with minor expenses and inconveniences.

When Bernie proposed this new system at a routine meeting of the counseling staff, he felt the reception was lukewarm and reserved. He was ready to provide a demonstration of how the new system would work. The counselors, however, indicated they did not have time. They acknowledged that his ideas were good, but they were only willing to discuss his system after they had time to review a written system description that had been approved by management.

Bernie was also surprised at the reaction of agency managers at their weekly meeting. The managers were more derisive. One joked that Bernie's hobby had become an obsession that wouldn't be satisfied until everything within the agency was computerized. Another teased that Bernie was addicted to his computer and wanted everyone else to be similarly hooked. The managers decided to form a special committee which included board members and an outside consultant to look into Bernie's suggestions. The managers were also not interested in seeing Bernie's demonstration.

Bernie approached the Executive Director to discuss what could be done to expedite the special committee study. Bernie was surprised to find the Executive Director expressed concerns about the cost of the system. He knew that funds were available. He also knew that the Executive Director understood that an outlay of $10,000 was inexpensive compared to what other agencies paid for similar systems. The Executive Director suggested that Bernie wait until the special committee reported its findings in 6 to 8 months. In the meantime, the Executive Director suggested that Bernie might like to computerize a volunteer scheduling system. Bernie requested time off and a small budget for this computerization effort. Nevertheless, the Executive Director stated that he could not delegate any of Bernie's normal duties to others without causing resentment. He thought he might find a thousand dollars for Bernie to spend on the volunteer system, if Bernie could get another computer donated.

Bernie was hurt. He had spent personal time developing a system which all agreed was successful. He had proposed changes that would eliminate management problems and move the agency into the information age. His proposals were sound and their costs reasonable. Yet, his ideas did not receive the serious consideration they deserved.

Bernie decided to take the day off and go fishing. During the day, these thoughts kept racing through his mind. Had he failed? If so, how had he failed? Was part of the negative reaction a response to the way he proposed the computer system, or was it related to the proposed system itself? What should be his next step? Should he spend extra time to develop the volunteer system, or was his energy and expertise being misused? Would another successful system give his proposal more credibility? Did he fail or was he stuck in an agency which preferred to live in the past? Finally, should he find a job at an agency that appreciated his insights and knowledge of computer-based information management?

Questions

1. How would you answer Bernie's questions in the final paragraph?

2. What does change theory tell us about Bernie's approach to computerization? Which principles about why and how people change did Bernie violate? What additionally could Bernie have done to prepare the agency for his proposed change?

3. What mandate and sanction did Bernie have for the system *he* developed? For the system and changes *he* proposed the agency make?

4. Should Bernie have involved others more in the computerization process, and if so, how?

5. Should major agency changes, such as redesigning the client record, be made before, after, or during computerization?

6. Should systems which involve information that cuts across programs be developed differently from systems which involve information within one program?

7. Are special safeguards required to protect the collection and use of potentially sensitive data such as work load measures?

CASE FOUR

New Kid on the Block

Michelle Morris had been Director of the Community Mental Health Center for 2 years. She assumed this position when the previous Director, Bernadine Johnson, retired. The previous Director had been satisfactory as an administrator, but had really always been, at heart, a caseworker. She was not a charismatic leader, and was unable to develop community and professional linkages with other agencies. In addition, her relationship with the board had been polite, but the members of the board were never overwhelmingly supportive. She did not feel it necessary to "play politics" as she called it, and was never able to build the board into a meaningful working unit. She was unable to do long-term planning, and thus everyone was relieved when she left.

Michelle's style was very different from the previous Director's, although she too had been a caseworker. She used a familial approach to working with the staff and board. She helped set up board retreats, where the board worked hard over a period of days developing long-term strategic plans for the agency. She brought little gifts for her secretary, and occasionally took her to lunch. She also developed a tradition of taking staff to lunch on their birthdays and instituted other times for get-togethers in the office. She was very low-key as a leader, and tried to make friends of her staff. This made it difficult to evaluate and talk to them as a supervisor when difficulties arose in the agency. Michelle carried a few cases to let her caseworkers know that she was still "in touch" with what the line workers were doing.

In some ways, Michelle was well-meaning, but she was not a good administrator. The agency had grant funds, and even though they were accountable for the grant monies, she felt that she should be able to spend the money in the agency as she saw fit, not as mandated by the funding source. Her bookkeeper had very little experience in nonprofit organizations, and Michelle, not a book-keeper, decided which accounts money should be placed in. An audit was done in the agency, and while not being accused of criminal wrongdoing, Michelle was strongly urged to resign by the board. The board members liked her personally, but as they were on the verge of losing a big grant due to her mismanagement, they felt as though they must think of the agency's survival first. At the same time, they did not want to lose someone thought so highly of by staff and board, so they offered to let her resign her position as Director, but stay on in a casework capacity. At first, Michelle was incensed and threatened to sue the board and the agency. She started looking for another job, but after a few months was still unable to find one. This was mainly due to the fact that the agency problems were well known in the social work community. Eventually, she agreed to resign and take a demotion to caseworker. A search was begun for a new Director.

John Simms was hired by the board after a search of qualified professionals in the area. He had experience as a caseworker, and had been Assistant Director of a family service agency in his last job. While a majority of the Board supported his appointment as Director, a small vocal group were still loyal to Michelle. They knew it was important for the agency to appear as though it were trying to "clean house," yet at the same time they felt she was being scapegoated for her assistant's incompetence.

Even before John arrived, there was trouble at the agency. Not only a few of the board members, but most of the caseworkers thought that Michelle's demotion was unfair. They felt that she had made a simple mistake, and that she was being treated in this manner partly due to sexism. In her low-key way, she was the leader of a formidable clique that could present John with numerous obstacles to any kind of change efforts.

When John arrived at the agency to start his new job, he was met by polite coldness on the part of the staff. His secretary had been very close to the old Director and while not actively hostile, she did not go out of her way to make him feel welcome. She had not even placed any office supplies in his office on his first day so that he had to go and ask her for pens, paper, envelopes, and a calendar. The caseworkers were wary of him and no one came and invited him to lunch.

Most of the board, on the other hand, were anxious to get the agency moving again and were supportive of him. John was familiar with what had happened in the agency and was concerned with his relationship with a staff person who had formerly been Director. He felt that it was a very awkward situation, and while the optimum condition would have been one in which the former Director was no longer present, he knew he had no choice in the matter.

He could see that the staff were a cohesive group and that he was an outsider. Some of the problems he knew he faced in trying to reshape the group into his team were that his leadership style was very different than his predecessor. He was more of a task-oriented leader. While he felt comfortable in small groups, he was extremely uncomfortable speaking in front of large groups. He was also a male with a largely female staff, and knew that he would have to be careful so that his overtures to friendship would not be misinterpreted. For example, while the previous Director could take staff to lunch and exchange little gifts with them, he knew that this could be interpreted as sexual harassment if he did this. His secretary still maintained much loyalty to her old boss, and even consulted with her regarding agency business. This could create numerous problems for him, especially if she shared confidential information with the old Director.

John knew that he could not move the agency forward until he dealt with the powerful informal groups in his agency. He needed to develop a strategy. On his second week on the job, he sat down in his office and thought about the three groups that he perceived to be affecting his new position: the board members still allied with the previous Director, the caseworkers who were part of her clique, and the secretarial staff who controlled the flow of important information in and out of the agency.

Questions

1. What kind of strategy should John develop to deal with each of these groups?

2. What do you think the relative importance of each of these groups in the agency is?

3. How important is it for administrators to be aware of informal groups in an agency? How does one find out about such groups?

CASE FIVE

ફ્ર

Breaking Up Is Hard to Do

Social Service Agency (SSA) is a sectarian family service agency that provides individual, family, and group counseling in a mid-sized city (under 500,000 population). It also provides family life education and other public service education programs to the community. Founded by its major funding source, a sectarian fundraising and allocating organization called the Community Planning Agency (CPA) of Pennington County, SSA remains a division of CPA rather than a separate agency because of the size of the community and lack of resources for it to function independently.

The Executive Director of the CPA is also the Director of the Social Service Agency. Thus the CPA Director is required to be an MSW as well as have extensive fundraising experience. However, in practice the SSA is actually run by the Associate Director, who is also an MSW, because the Executive Director is always so busy with the annual campaign. An Advisory Board of twenty persons from the community operates as a quasi-legal board to the SSA, although all final decisions are made by the CPA Board.

Jim Hollings, the Associate Director of the Social Services Agency, has become increasingly frustrated by the complexities of operations because of the lack of autonomy of the agency. He is also frustrated by having to report to a Director who shows very little interest in the agency. Jim feels that he is, in fact, running the agency, but all the credit is going to Arthur Bloom, the Executive Director. Jim has talked to sympathetic members of his Advisory Board. At the last Advisory Board meeting, a committee was formed to explore the possibility of the Social Services Agency separating from its parent organization. Three Board members were appointed along with Jim to serve on this committee and make recommendations to the Board of the CPA. The following is a report of their findings:

INTRODUCTION

In gathering information for this report, a number of people were consulted, including Advisory Board members of the Social Service Agency, Board members of the CPA, the Executive Director of a similar sized family service agency in Metro City, community leaders, and the Executive Director of the CPA.

THE ISSUES

The separation of the Social Service Agency from the CPA involves a great many considerations. There are legal, financial, political, and other issues in such an undertaking. What follows is a synopsis of some of these concerns.

1. Identity Issues

Many of the informants whom we consulted feel that the Social Service Agency is not a recognizable entity in the community and that even one of its major funding sources, The United Way, is confused by the present arrangement. Because of this lack of identity, many people in the community are not aware of the existence of SSA. Those who are aware of it are not sure what it does. If the Social Service Agency became a separate legal entity the public would be better able to differentiate it and its services from its parent organization, the CPA. Becoming a separate organization would help clarify the role and function of the Agency in the community as well as attract more volunteers to help in its work.

On the other hand, some view the present arrangement as a way for the CPA to deliver direct services to the community; retain tighter control of the agency, its budget, its services, and ensure quality of services.

2. *Legal Issues*

At the present time the Social Service Agency has no assets, while the CPA has numerous assets. One of the major advantages of separating the Agency from the CPA is that it relieves the CPA of liability from actions of the SSA and its staff. This means that any potential lawsuit against the SSA, whether a malpractice claim or personal injury claim, would not threaten the assets of the CPA. It also means that the CPA Board would not be liable for SSA actions.

An advantage for SSA of separation is that it would be a separate legal entity and could obtain liability insurance for its Board. At the present time SSA has an advisory committee that acts as a board, but is unable to obtain board insurance because it does not meet the legal requirements of a Board.

A disadvantage to SSA would be that it would lose whatever legal protection it now enjoys by being under the umbrella of the CPA.

Some informants that we spoke with expressed concern about the possible loss to the CPA of a municipal property tax exemption due to the loss of its direct service component. However, neither SSA nor CPA have any property, thus property tax is not an issue at the present time. It may become an issue at a future date if the CPA decides to buy the building it is currently leasing.

3. *Financial Issues*

There are a great many financial considerations involved in any separation of the two entities. Some of these are as follows:

A. *Funding:* One advantage of separation to SSA would be that the Agency could secure alternative sources of funds through its own fundraising efforts, receiving gifts directly, and other means. As the Agency actually provides services, it would attract contributors who would prefer to give directly to it without having the money go through a third party.

Furthermore, raising money through the grant review process would be easier since SSA's identity would be clearer.

A disadvantage to SSA is the possibility that the community cannot support a separate agency at this time. Nevertheless, many respondents noted that there are a myriad of other sources, including state and federal contracts for services, that could be tapped to bolster revenues for the Agency.

A perceived disadvantage to CPA is that it would be competing with SSA for limited community resources, and thus stands to lose donations in its own campaign because funds would be diverted to SSA. This has not usually been the case with other allocation agencies, such as United Ways, which have guidelines for member agencies regarding community fundraising activities.

An advantage to CPA is that SSA, its board, and volunteers, could become active participants in the CPA's annual campaign.

B. Costs: The present Executive Director of CPA is willing to guarantee for a specified period of time that he would continue in his present capacity. An advantage of this arrangement would be that SSA would not require funds for additional executive salaries. A disadvantage of this arrangement might be that other funding sources, as well as other agencies and organizations funded by the CPA, would perceive the Executive Director's dual role as a conflict of interest, especially if SSA might be given special consideration in allocation of funds.

Eventually, SSA will require its own full-time Executive Director and this will increase costs for salaries and fringes. This perceived burden is outweighed by the potential advantage of having an Executive who could devote the time needed to market and raise funds for the agency through grant-writing, contracting, and development activities.

In any case, there would be other immediate increased costs to the agency if it lost its present status. Some of these costs include incorporation costs, office space, clerical staff, equipment, furnishings, and so forth.

4. Autonomy Issues

If SSA were a separate agency it would have more independence of action, more freedom to set its own goals and policies. It would have more room to grow and flourish, to become more creative. Indeed, separation would force it to be more creative in order to better serve the community and attract the resources needed to survive on its own.

A disadvantage of this autonomy is that SSA would have to apply for allocations in the same manner as any other agency with no guaranteed level of funding. It would have to present its budget and compete for funding in a harsh economic environment.

5. Organizational Issues

Having a separate organization may mean that SSA would be able to operate more efficiently as it would shed its present bureaucratic structural overlay. For example, some of our respondents commented that the kind of issues that come to SSA should not have to go through the CAP board. It would simplify the organizational structure by decreasing the number of decision-making levels.

6. Growth Issues

Most people we talked to agreed that SSA needed to expand services, staff, and quarters, as they were all inadequate at the present time. Nevertheless, the question of how this expansion would be paid for is a primary concern.

7. Other Issues

Other important issues that have been raised relate to board ownership and leadership development in the community. If SSA had its own board, it would be able to serve some important functions for the agency that most other boards serve, such as advocating and fundraising. Having its own separate board would also mean that SSA could serve as a training ground for future community leaders.

Table 5.1 illustrates the current organizational structure of SSA and its relationship to CPA. Table 5.2 shows the proposed organizational structure of SSA.

Questions
ᴥ

1. If you were Jim Hollings, what would you recommend regarding the separation of the two agencies and why?

Table 5.1 Current Organizational Chart of Social Service Agency, Inc.

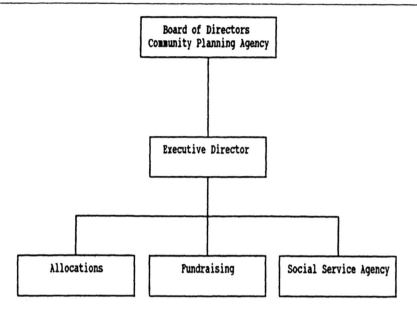

Table 5.2 Proposed Organizational Structure of Social Service Agency, Inc.

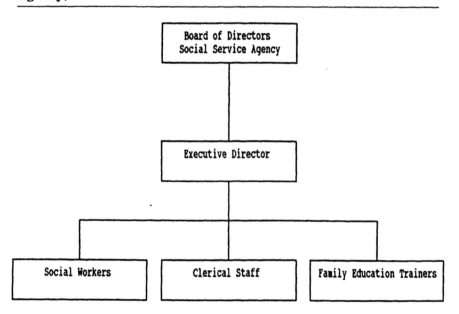

2. How would you present your recommendation to the CPA Board to maximize a positive vote for your case?

3. What do you see as the major advantages and disadvantages of separation to both agencies?

4. If separation were not recommended, in what other ways could the Social Service Agency simplify its present complex decisionmaking structure?

CASE SIX

ᕰ

The Rice War

The Southwest Training Institute, a nonprofit corporation, was originally established to develop curriculum content for schools of social work on the delivery of mental health services to Hispanics. This curriculum content was presented to social work educators in workshops, seminars, and conferences conducted by the Institute's Executive Director and his training staff in various locations throughout the country. Headquartered in Houston, STI was almost totally dependent upon federal grants for its existence. Realizing that federal funding for training would not last indefinitely, and wanting to establish STI as a permanent institution, the Institute's Board of Directors decided to broaden the agency's funding base through diversification of program operations. It directed the Executive Director to explore any and all areas of relevant program expansion.

A year after the Board's directive, the Houston Community Council published the results of a needs assessment of low-income neighborhoods in the city. Among other things, it identified a number of unmet social needs in a Hispanic barrio known as Magnolia. The Council's report also revealed that the Magnolia area was not being served by any of the United Way Agencies, and that no private or public agency was located even near this relatively new and rapidly growing Mexican American enclave.

At the next quarterly meeting of the STI Board of Directors, a decision was made to begin diversifying by creating a social service component to address the needs of the Magnolia area Hispanics. The Board directed STI's Executive Director to maintain the Institute's national training thrust while concomitantly developing a local Hispanic multiservice agency. Approximately nine months later, sufficient state and local funds had been secured to establish a family and drug abuse counseling component of STI in Magnolia to be known as El Centro de Familias.

Hiring bilingual and bicultural professional counseling staff did not present a problem. There were enough Chicano MSWs working in mainstream agencies in Houston who gladly left their jobs to participate in the creation of the city's first professionally staffed Mexican American social work agency. Within weeks after funds were received, the Executive Director had hired a program director and five clinicians.

The problem was in finding suitable office space in a barrio of substandard housing and a less than adequate infrastructure. A site, however, was finally located. It consisted of a two-bedroom frame house with an attached garage which had been enlarged and converted into a tortilla "factory." It had one bathroom, and air conditioning was provided by two window AC units. Although far from luxurious, and in no way comparable to STI's central office, a seven-room modern office suite, the small house was turned into office space suitable for the purposes of the program.

The formal behavior of the two STI professional staffs—the trainers and the El Centro clinicians—were, from the start, differentially determined according to respective functions. Trainers, for example, did not keep rigid business hours, except when on training missions. Except for attendance at supervisory conferences, staff meetings, and training "dry-runs," trainers were free to do research in any of the several university libraries in the city. Workshop preparation was usually done in the office, sometimes late into the night. Moreover, training involved traveling, often long distances, to conduct two-to-three day sessions, many on weekends.

El Centro staff, on the other hand, were expected to be in the office from 9 to 5, and to regularly see clients one night per week, and on Saturdays. Travel consisted of one, perhaps two, professional conferences per year.

When not conducting training, trainers were free to dress as they pleased. Clinicians, on the other hand, were expected to dress professionally during office hours.

There were other disparities in working conditions. Trainers worked in a well appointed, modern office building with underground parking, close to trendy eateries and fashionable shopping malls.

Clinicians, by contrast, worked in cramped, dilapidated quarters, parked curbside on semi-paved streets, and rarely had time to eat lunch anywhere other than the two or three neighborhood Mexican restaurants.

Finally, there was the matter of staffs' accessibility to the Executive Director, George. Except at monthly staff meetings held at the STI central office, or during George's biweekly supervisory conferences with El Centro's program director, clinicians rarely had an opportunity to interact with him. Yet George was almost in constant contact with the trainers, both at the central office and on the road.

One area in which there were no disparities was in salaries, which were identical at the entry level. That trainers earned more than clinicians was based on the former's longer tenure with the organization.

Approximately one year after El Centro opened, friction between training and clinical staff began to surface. Conflict was first noted in monthly staff meetings, and consisted of mild barbs hurled at each other in thinly disguised jocular terms related to differences in work schedules, travel opportunities, time spent with "the boss," office facilities, etc. That the director of counseling was a main participant in this exchange only served to fuel the increasingly hostile side remarks interjected during these meetings.

The seriousness of the conflict was not lost upon the Executive Director. After considerable thought, he decided that the way to handle the friction between the two staffs would be to hold a retreat away from the office in an informal and relaxed setting where both groups could focus on total agency mission and goals, while at the same time having an opportunity to better understand and appreciate each other's work, and to get better acquainted personally.

All staff greeted the idea of a retreat enthusiastically. A joint clinician-trainer committee, chaired by the Executive Director, was appointed to plan the retreat, including the selection of a site, the living arrangements, the business agenda, and after-hours social activities. The committee decided on a 3-day meeting in a popular resort in the hill country. A condominium large enough to house the entire staff, with a fully equipped kitchen and several bedrooms, was reserved, as was a large conference room in the main building of the resort facility. Two of the counselors, Joe and Magda, volunteered to develop the three-day menu, and staff signed up for kitchen duty — cooking, serving, cleaning, and marketing.

Traveling in a convoy consisting of two vans, the entire STI staff — clinicians, trainers, and support staff (12 in all; four men and eight women) — arrived at the resort on a pleasant Thursday afternoon, in time to unpack and take advantage of the facility's amenities. The Executive Director was pleased that clinicians and trainers co-mingled as they went off to play tennis, to swim, play basketball, or simply walk along the idyllic brook fronting the condominium. Dinner the first evening was prepared by Joe and Magda, according to their preplanned menu. It consisted of broiled chicken and Spanish rice.

After breakfast the following morning, staff met in the conference room to begin developing organizational goals and objectives for the coming fiscal year. Try as he might to get staff interested in total agency goals, the Executive Director was able to generate only perfunctory participation by trainers in discussing service goals and by counselors in helping to formulate training goals. The overt camaraderie present during the first day of the retreat seemed to be abating. After lunch, prepared by two support staff and consisting of, among other things, Spanish rice, as per Joe and Magda's menu, the staff reconvened in the conference room. Even before goals and objectives had been determined, a number of the counselors starting raising questions about plans to secure more suitable office space for El Centro. They complained about the landlord's unresponsiveness to breakdowns in the air conditioning and plumbing equipment, rat and roach infestation, and building security. One counselor wondered if money spent on the retreat might not have been more wisely used to improve working conditions at El Centro. In rejoinder, a trainer noted that funds spent for the retreat were from a discretionary account built up over the years by extra, non-grant related training activities conducted by trainers above and beyond grant requirements. Efforts by the Executive Director to refocus the group's attention on the determination of agency goals and objectives fell on deaf ears. The meeting was adjourned early by the Executive Director with an exhortation to both trainers and counselors to cool down and return the following morning prepared to address the broader issues facing the agency.

The preparation of that evening's meal devolved to Gina, one of the trainers, and to the Executive Director, George. She looked at the menu and through clenched teeth hissed, "What? We're having Spanish rice again? We've had rice for every meal except breakfast. I'll be damned if I make rice tonight. Enough is enough." George merely said, "You're the cook."

Dinner time was announced and staff sat around the dining table as Gina and George brought out the platters of food. After all the plates were laid out and everyone had sat down, Joe and Magda, almost in unison, and certainly in anger, exclaimed "Where is the rice?" Gina calmly retorted: "Not tonight. Not while I'm cook. You want rice, you go make it!"

Magda turned to George. "Did you authorize this change in the menu?" "It's no big deal, Magda. What's to authorize? So we don't have rice again. What's the problem?" he replied.

"As far as I'm concerned," responded Magda angrily, "it is a very big deal, and the problem is you. You always take their side against us. Joe and I spent a lot of time preparing the menu, which everyone approved. Now, without consulting us, you let Gina change it. This is just another indication of how things are done in this agency. You always side with your 'training team.' And now you insult us by having one of 'your' trainers change a menu which we had all approved. I've had it!"

Needless to say, all of the actual or conjectured animosities between the two staffs erupted into full-blown arguments. And staff relations deteriorated accordingly.

Questions
ra.

1. What are the possible sources of conflict leading to the "rice war"?

2. Why did the agency retreat fail to resolve the agency's internal conflict?

3. What are possible alternative solutions to this type of intra-organizational conflict?

CASE SEVEN

ॐ

Which Side Are You On?

"Things really need to change here."
"Change keeps an agency alive. We haven't changed in
5 years and are slowly disintegrating."
"The new executive will have to clean house."

These were typical of the statements Pam heard before the new executive director arrived. As a newly appointed supervisor, Pam and other staff had concluded that the former executive director had retired five years too late. The retiring executive director had been a strong leader for 15 years. He had brought the agency from its small beginnings to a multi-service organization with a staff of fifty. Five years before, the agency's reputation had been excellent. Weak management, however, could be seen in a lack of new initiatives and creative approaches to client problems. The agency had become a follower rather than a leader. This stagnation was beginning to effect the agency's reputation in the community.

Internally, the lack of strong leadership resulted in several program directors building autonomous power centers. The agency now had many uncoordinated programs, each competing for agency resources and pulling the agency apart. Also, the philosophy on which the agency was founded had been outgrown. The agency was missing a core purpose and values that could guide it through continual changes in funding and service philosophy.

Changing the agency with the old executive director at the helm was impossible. He had lost interest and was out of touch. While some board members were concerned, many of the original board members remained. They would not make changes that would upset or tarnish the reputation of the old Executive Director before his retirement.

The new Executive Director was welcomed by all. She was hired because she demonstrated strong leadership capabilities. Pam liked her personally, but felt she lacked many of the social skills of the old executive. The new executive began making changes immediately. Everyone realized that a few of the changes they advocated for would probably occur. They also realized that changes their rivals wanted might occur along with many changes no one anticipated or wanted. The situation was similar to the problem of tax reform. Everyone favors tax reform. Reform is only popular, however, when it means keeping one's own tax deductions while eliminating the deductions of others. In the agency, everyone was fighting to keep the power they had gained from the weak retiring executive. With each change, however, the new executive consolidated more power over agency programs.

Within the last months, the situation had gradually moved from dissatisfaction to insurrection. Those with power finally realized that the only way not to lose power and control over their programs was to ban together and revolt. Clandestine meetings were held during work and after hours. Each change by the new executive was discussed not in terms of how it would help the agency, but in terms of how it could be blocked. Program directors were having private discussions with sympathetic agency board members, and rumors were surfacing about new proposed changes that appeared ridiculous to most staff. Morale was getting worse. Some disgruntled staff had found better jobs while others were circulating their resume to see what jobs were available. Those cooperating with the executive became suspect, even if they were old friends. The agency was divided, with everyone being pressured to be for or against the new executive. Client services were beginning to suffer as internal politics took more and more of the staff's time and energy.

Pam had attended a meeting of 11 concerned staff the previous evening to discuss the situation and what could be done about it. After hearing some new revelations from several program directors, she became convinced that many of the changes were destroying rather than rebuilding the agency. Everyone present voted to oppose the destructive changes. Everyone was instructed to think about ways to prevent the new executive from making the undesired changes, before the following week's meeting. Many were talking about ways to get rid of the new executive. After the meeting, Pam feared that a mutiny was taking place and that she might have become part of it.

While Pam was thinking about all this, the new executive walked in her office and asked her if she could talk to her. Startled, Pam said yes and the new executive closed the door. The executive stated that since her arrival, she had been impressed with Pam's work, her ability to listen, and her willingness to see both sides of an issue. She also stated that she admired the trust that existed between Pam and her workers. She confided to Pam about some of the tough decisions she was having to make and the resistance that she was receiving. She felt that while she may not have explained her changes well, those wanting to hold onto old ways had purposefully misinterpreted her intentions. She was upset about all the turmoil, but felt it was unavoidable due to the long absence of strong leadership. She indicated she had taken the job with a mandate from the board and staff to make all necessary changes to bring the agency back to its former prominence. She said she would make those changes and was strong enough to overcome any consequences. She would not be intimidated by those attempting to hold onto their power at the expense of the whole agency.

To Pam's horror, the new executive then began asking questions about the meeting the night before. She said she knew basically who attended and what had occurred. She wanted to know if Pam agreed with the others, or if she could trust Pam to support the changes necessary to get the agency back on track. She indicated that Pam had to either be for her or against her. Then she paused, and asked Pam for her views.

Questions

1. How does a new executive develop a vision of the agency's mission and get agency staff to buy into that mission?

2. What could the new executive have done to prevent this situation from evolving as it did?

3. Is it unethical or unprofessional for agency staff to meet privately with board members on internal issues before presenting these issues internally through established channels?

4. Is it unethical or unprofessional for the new executive to force Pam to take sides?

5. If you were Pam, what would you do?

6. If you were the new executive in this situation, what would you do now?

Henri
Fayol

Chain of Command

Unity of Purpose

CASE EIGHT

ew

The Battered Women's Shelter
of Aiken County

The Battered Women's Shelter of Aiken County has been in existence for 15 years. Its mission is to provide a safe, temporary, emergency shelter for female victims of domestic violence and their children. In addition to emergency shelter, other services provided include adult and children's counseling, information and referral services, transportation, and emergency medical assistance. It is the only shelter in a county that is a mix of rural farming areas and small towns. The shelter was first established in a small trailer on a lot donated by a church. Two years later, a large five-bedroom house was purchased. Seven years after that, a 64-resident facility was completed. Last year 337 women and 487 children were sheltered. The average length of stay is 6 weeks.

Most of the current board members of the Shelter have been involved with the agency since its inception. They worked hard to raise money for it, they oversaw the first building, and they have continued to play many different roles in the organization. In fact, some work as volunteers at the shelter during the week in addition to their board responsibilities.

There are 22 members of the Board of Directors, up to 30 are allowed by the agency's by-laws. There are also 12 full-time staff and two part-time staff. There are 55 active volunteers (22 of them from the Board) donating an average total of 500 volunteer hours a month. Board members volunteer an average of three to 60 hours per month at the agency. Volunteers work with children, work in adult group sessions, answer the hotline, do yard maintenance, transport clients, and are involved in community relations and fundraising.

The by-laws of the agency state that:

1. A volunteer program shall be established under the direction of a Volunteer Coordinator.

2. The Executive Director may appoint a Volunteer Coordinator (who may be but need not be, a member of the Board of Directors) with the approval of the Board of Directors who shall serve under the supervision and control of the Executive Director.

This active involvement of the board members in the day-to-day operations in the agency is what has led to the current problem. Merilee Abrams, a board member who works at the house twice a week as the Volunteer Coordinator, is one of the founding members of the Shelter Board. She has spent a good part of the last 15 years trying to build the shelter as a safe, comfortable place for mothers and their children fleeing abusive situations. Because she has been so involved in the shelter, she is also highly critical and vocal when staff do things she does not approve of. She may call them to task publicly or she may go directly to the Executive Director, often reminding her that she, Merilee, is her boss. Because of her overinvolvement in what she perceives to be "her agency," staff have been harassed or pressured to resign when she disagreed with their handling of client families, or if she had a personality conflict with one of them. This has created a situation in which the director is being constantly undermined by board members because staff know that a board member working that day may make a decision without consulting the director until after the fact.

The by-laws of the agency state that:

> Directors shall be elected to serve 3 years, with one-third (1/3) to be elected each year. Directors may serve no more than two consecutive terms.

Some of the board members, such as Merilee, serve two consecutive terms then rotate off the board for a year. They are then elected again to serve on the board for two more terms because of their dedication and hard work as volunteers in the program. Merilee also has extensive community contacts that have been helpful in securing funding and corporate sponsorship for the agency.

Some of the newer members of the Board have heard complaints from staff and clients about Board members such as Merilee, about their "meddling" in staff and client business. They feel that the Board should play a different role in the agency, that their role is to oversee, not run the agency. But Merilee and some of the other long-term Board members feel that these new Board members do not have the emotional investment, the "sweat equity" that she and the others have. She cannot sit idly by and delegate the operations of the agency to staff who might not care as much as she does.

The anger and resentment caused by Merilee's constant intrusions into day-to-day operations finally came to a head when Merilee accused the Outreach Coordinator of incompetence and asked for her resignation. Usually her next tactic would be to call the President of the Board, explain her position, garner his support, then inform the Executive Director. The Outreach Coordinator refused to resign and went to the Executive Director for her support.

Questions

1. What should be the proper role of a board of directors?

2. What should be the relationship of staff to the board?

3. What would you do as executive director of this agency about the intrusions of board members in day-to-day operations?

4. How would you handle this incident?

CASE NINE

❧

Planning and the Politics of Inclusion

Fontaine H. Fulghum

The newly elected Mayor of a large, economically-distressed metropolitan area in the Southeast is concerned with making good his campaign promises with respect to economic development, maintaining racial and ethnic harmony, and building a responsive human service delivery system. He appoints a "blue ribbon" panel of experts from local universities and industry to address economic development and strengthening the City's Human Relations Council to address issues stemming from cultural diversity. He then turns to his Cabinet for approaches to better meet human needs in the city.

The directors of the City Departments of Health, of Welfare, and of Policy Planning, as well as key planning staff attached to the Mayor's Office, are in agreement that the City has no established authority for the coordination of human services. With the exception of running several human services institutions under city charter since the days of the "poor laws" and almshouses, the city has had no real role in or responsibility for meeting human need.

This arena, the Mayor is told, is instead the province of the State, and that agent of the State, the County. This is so despite the fact that most of those citizens of the County who are poor and oppressed, and therefore most in need of services, reside in the City. City staffers also note that the private sector, particularly United Way, several responsive corporations, and a number of foundations are involved in generating and allocating dollars to meet specified human need. Nevertheless, no unified, plan-driven, system could be identified under any auspice.

The Mayor reiterates that building a responsive human service delivery system remained a major priority of his administration, for reasons of good politics as well as good public policy. He asks the Policy Planning Department to make recommendations to him within thirty days as to how the City might get a "handle" on human services and begin to shape a policy and a plan for strategic use of resources in this vital area.

Accordingly, the Policy Planning staff recommend that the Farris Family Foundation and two major development corporations be approached to fund a comprehensive human services needs assessment, the first such effort in the City's history. It is also suggested that at the same time, negotiations be undertaken with the State to secure, under contract, the responsibility by the City for allocating those Social Security Block Grant [SSBG] funds currently expended in the City by the State for the purchase of social services to children, needy families, and the elderly. Combined with those Community Development Block Grant funds the City already controls, the City would then potentially be positioned to fund some unmet needs and redirect resources according to the outcomes of the needs assessment.

Although the Chief of Policy Planning, Gayle Goodwin, has received the Mayor's approval of the strategy, she remains concerned about nascent "turf" issues. The Area Agency on Aging is charged with planning for services for persons in the County who are aged sixty and over. The Metropolitan United Way recently disbanded its planning affiliate and is struggling with a new structure for its allocation process. Protestant Charities has announced its intention to study the needs of a recent influx of Asian refugees. While Policy Planning staff lean toward bringing in a team of specialists in needs assessment from an Eastern university, Ms. Goodwin remains mindful of local parochialism and of the Mayor's penchant for task forces. She is also a firm believer that needs assessment is necessarily a consensus building, as well as a research-based, enterprise.

The resulting Mayor's Task Force on Human Need is launched with a breakfast meeting at the Petroleum Club hosted by the Mayor. It consists of key human services decision-makers, public and private. Attending, and committed to personally participate in the process, are the State Commissioner of Human Services [as the State sees this as an innovative project], the County Superintendent of Schools, the presiding Judge of the Family Court, the Chairman of Metropolitan United Way, the President of the Area Agency on Aging, the heads of the largest service provider agencies and the

Chairs of both the Junior League and the Welfare Rights Association. Protestant Charities has declined to participate, and a board member of Church Women United is asked to take the seat thus vacated.

The leadership group assembled at the Petroleum Club discusses plans for an inclusive structure to address concerns of various subpopulations. At the same time, at a Press Conference across town, a disgruntled Protestant Charities official, and a city councilman whose district has been impacted by the recent influx of refugees, decry the Administration's "power grab" and "attempt to control the city's underclass." Fredric Rohatyn, the Executive Director of Protestant Charities, until recently the President of Developing World Missions, Inc., has issued a statement to the press likening the City to a third world country and the Mayor to a dictator supported by a military-industrial junta.

The afternoon papers are largely supportive of the city's effort to re-order what is viewed as the human services "quagmire." The councilman is characterized by the *Gazette* as "opportunistic"; his plans to run against the Mayor in four years are well known. Protestant Charities is described by the *Observer* as "well-intentioned but naive." However, the leading daily in the state Capitol suggests that the Mayor, despite his "strong community savvy," may have "chosen the wrong issue."

Back at City Hall, when his Chief of Staff asks the Mayor how to handle "those irascible fellows at Protestant Charities", the Mayor tells him characteristically to "draw a circle that takes them in." The politics of inclusion and the technology of planning continue in tandem as the City addresses human need.

Questions

i.

1. Do human service practitioners have a role to play in placing human need as a priority item on the public policy agenda? Who was responsible for doing that here?

2. Was the City's strategy for establishing a role in planning for human services a sound one? Why should a municipality be concerned about "having a handle" on addressing human need?

3. Was the "inclusionary" approach a good one? Why was there dissent from some parties in the City? Do you think it was justified?

4. Do you agree with Ms. Goodwin that needs assessment is a consensus-building process, or is it primarily a research effort? Support your answer.

5. Does the scrutiny planning is subject to in the public domain increase accountability or simply generate discord? What are the results here?

About the Case Author
ðø

Fontaine H. Fulghum, MSW, is a management consultant with over 20 years experience in human services planning and administration, which she has taught in the Schools of Social Work at Tulane University and Rutgers University.

CASE TEN

≥∢

The Hit Man

As Director of the City's Social Services Department (SSD), Mike Mason has weathered several storms with the City Council over the past nine years; mostly over money. Whereas the City has grown, and so has the number of indigent residents, the Council has not increased its appropriation to SSD commensurately. The consequences are that the agency's clients are getting smaller emergency grants while the costs for rent and food have increased. While few clients complain directly to City Hall, complaints from landlords not getting a full subsidy or getting it late have escalated to the point that several of the City Council members have demanded an explanation from Mike about the "state of affairs" at SSD.

Mike appeared before City Council to defend his department by pointing out that the problem was not the state of affairs of SSD but the reluctance of City Hall to adequately fund the department and to streamline its payment policies so that clients and landlords would get sufficient and timely assistance. He accused the Council, including the Mayor and two newly elected Council members, of being more concerned about absentee landlords not getting paid on time than about the needs of the city's indigent population.

While several people in the social welfare community applauded Mike's candor and temerity at the Council meeting, others wondered about the wisdom of Mike criticizing his bosses in public, especially during an election year.

At the next Council meeting, the Mayor, John Lindell, and the two new Council members, Marcia Cisneros and Harold Dobrinski,

73

out-voted the other two Council members, Henry B. Stovall and Bubba Baker on a motion made by Cisneros to hire a consultant to conduct a management audit of the Social Services Department. Mayor Lindell ordered the City Attorney, Jane Hyatt, to contract with a consultant of her choice to conduct the audit and to notify the Advisory Board and Director of SSD that such an audit would take place. Councilman Baker, who had been on the council when Mike was hired as SSD director, and who had supported him over the years in trying to get the Council to increase its appropriations to the agency, adamantly objected to what he perceived as an attempt by Lindell, Cisneros, and Dobrinski to bring in a "hit man" to get rid of Mike. Predictably, the local newspaper headline the following day read: "'HIT MAN' TO REVIEW SSD."

City Attorney Hyatt consulted with a few close associates and acquaintances in trying to identify a person to conduct the management audit. She was eventually referred to the Director of the Community Planning Council, who suggested that an outsider be brought in — someone who had no local political ties and no personal stake in the outcome. He recommended a former college professor, Dr. Enrico, a management expert with years of experience in the human services, now retired and living in Los Alamos, New Mexico.

Dr. Enrico agreed to conduct the management audit, under the following terms and conditions: that he 1) be given access to each council member, all SSD staff, Advisory Board members, agency clients, and all other significant stakeholders related to SSD's operation; 2) be provided with all statistical and financial reports produced by SSD over the last 5 years; 3) be accorded secretarial services and office space while conducting the audit on site; and 4) be given four weeks in which to conduct the audit. A contract between the City and the consultant was drawn up according to mutually agreed terms and conditions and executed one week before the start of the audit. City Attorney Hyatt notified the City Council, the director of SSD, and the Advisory Board, of the inclusive dates of Dr. Enrico's program evaluation.

The first person Dr. Enrico contacted upon arriving in town was SSD Director Mike Mason. A meeting with Mike and his staff was set up for the following morning at 10:00 o'clock. Knowing the anxiety that program audits generate on the part of staff, Enrico wanted to address their concerns and answer their questions first thing. He knew as well that Mike would be apprehensive and therefore suggested a meeting with him prior to the meeting with staff.

Arriving at the agency at 8:30 A.M., Dr. Enrico was surprised to enter an empty waiting room. He introduced himself to the receptionist and asked for Mr. Mason. He also wondered why there were no clients in the reception area. The receptionist nervously replied that after the middle of the month few clients came in because they knew that the agency's monthly emergency assistance budget would have been expended. The few clients who did come in were interviewed by one of the six caseworkers and referred to other agencies.

Dr. Enrico was shown to Mike Mason's office, a spartan but comfortable room not far from the reception area. After introductions, Dr. Enrico noted the remarkable calm and quiet of the agency; he had expected lines of people coming to request help. Mike, a gaunt, bespeckled man of about 35, repeated in essence what the receptionist had said about the mid-month cut off point.

After meeting with the director, Enrico met, in Mike's presence, with his staff in a small, sparsely furnished conference room. It seemed obvious to the consultant from what he observed that the agency was not splurging on office amenities. As Enrico explained the purpose of the audit and the procedures entailed, staff remained reserved but politely attentive. He announced that he would be interviewing each staff person individually, and that all communication would be treated in the strictest confidence. The purpose of the audit, Dr. Enrico reminded them, was to enhance the agency's effectiveness and efficiency in the provision of services to clients. He acknowledged to the staff that the media had branded him as a "hit man" whose purpose was to help certain members of the City Council in getting rid of Mr. Mason as director. That, Dr. Enrico strongly specified, was not his agenda. His goal was to examine total agency operations, including the role and responsibilities of City Council in providing policy direction and fiscal support to the program, community perceptions of the agency's impact on the needs of the poor, client perceptions of the agency's sensitivity and response to their plight, and the agency's managerial and service delivery performance in providing emergency relief to its clients.

The ensuing weeks were spent in interviewing council members, agency representatives, clients, staff members, and in reviewing agency service and financial reports. Advisory Board members were also interviewed. In addition, Dr. Enrico and Mr. Mason had several long sessions regarding Mike's perceptions of agency operations.

Several things were discovered and contained in Dr. Enrico's report to the City Council. Among them were the following:

- Clients of SSD reported that they were treated with courtesy, helpfulness, and respect by caseworkers.

- Staff indicated loyalty and commitment toward the agency and its director.

- Directors and staff of community social service agencies viewed the City Council as insensitive to the needs of the poor.

- The Advisory Board was split in its support of the agency director: some viewed him as a functionary who had no leadership qualities; others said he was doing the best with what he had.

- The statistical and financial reports of the agency were in total disarray — to the point that it was impossible to determine how many clients had been served over the past five years at what cost.

- The City Council had neglected its City Charter duty to "closely monitor and review the operations of the Social Service Department and its Director on an ongoing and periodic basis" — the agency and its director had never been evaluated once in nine years.

- Except during times of crises, the City Council assumed no responsibility whatsoever for the direction of its Social Services Department, relying instead on its appointed but powerless SSD Advisory Board to fulfill the Council's legal obligation.

- The director of SSD was hired without the proper program and fiscal knowledge and skills to run the agency, but simply on the fact that he had been in a supervisory position in a local public agency and had political connections at City Hall. Nine years later, he hadn't developed the knowledge and skills and had lost the political connections.

In summary, the management audit report faulted the City Council for neglecting its policy-making and monitoring responsibilities toward its Social Services Department, and recommended that it delegate its oversight responsibility to the department's Advisory Board by empowering it as a Policy Board. The report made no recommendation as to the retention or firing of the agency's director. In that respect, the "hit man" deferred to the City Council.

Questions

1. What is the difference between a "program audit" and a "program outcome" or "program impact" evaluation?

2. Comment of the findings and recommendations of the program audit.

3. Discuss the pros and cons of the audit's silence on the retention or dismissal of the agency director.

CASE ELEVEN

?&

Staffing a Planning Committee

In her new job, Mary was responsible for staffing a 15-member Addictions Committee. She knew from the first day that she inherited some problems. The committee had met biweekly for the last year to work on an addictions plan that was due in three months. However, the committee had only gathered data and was unclear on how to translate the data into a plan. Mary had wanted to spend the first month on the job introducing herself to key community leaders to get a "feel of the territory." The pressure, however, was on to produce an approved addictions plan on time.

Committee members claimed exhaustion. Under the guidance of a student intern, whom they regarded fondly, the committee had painstakingly gathered addictions data from every imaginable source. They had 5 years' worth of data such as addiction arrests, court dispositions, and treatment admissions. They also had interviews with counselors, school principles, clergy, hospital administrators, and others who had opinions about the problem of addictions. When Mary asked what research questions they were trying to prove or disprove by collecting all the data, members indicated that was not their job, but her job. They had collected all the data because they knew it was important.

Mary felt that the first task was to eliminate the committee's weariness by cutting down on the number of meetings. Rather than meeting biweekly, she established three subcommittees, one to focus on alcohol, one on drugs, and another on addictive substances. These subcommittees would meet bimonthly and report at a quarterly meeting of all three Committees. This new structure could accomplish the same work while cutting the number of meetings each person attended from approximately 25 to 12 per year.

Mary's next task was to prepare the committee for the process of developing needs statements from the data and developing goals, objectives, and possible intervention strategies. The next committee meeting was spent developing a mission statement and guiding principles. With the guidance provided by the committee's mission and guiding principles, Mary put all the data into tables and charts. Then, trends and priority needs were identified by each subcommittee after analyzing the data. Possible intervention strategies, however, were not obvious from the data. A logical void existed between the desires and values of the mission statement and guiding principles and the data. Many of the principles had no data from which to determine if action was needed. For example, one guiding principle stressed preventive education by the family. No data, however, addressed current family-based prevention efforts. Even where principles had associated data, the data often did not point towards possible intervention strategies.

Mary's solution was to call an all day committee meeting at a pleasant, quiet hotel. Warmed by a fireplace and refreshments, the committee spent the morning discussing the data, the trends, and the needs supported by the data. In the afternoon, they began formulating goals, objectives, and possible intervention strategies. Mary's suspicions were true. The goals, objectives, and strategies were based more on the guiding principles than the data. Most goals and objectives had little supporting data. The committee, however, was pleased with their recommendations and was not bothered by the lack of supporting data. Mary then combined all the information into a final plan that all approved.

While the plan was considered a success, Mary noticed that some committee members were dissatisfied with the new meeting arrangement. They expressed dismay that they were not seeing each other very often and not having as much fun as before. Mary now realized that their complaints about overwork were not pleas for less work: they were to impress others and to obtain recognition for their volunteer effort. In her rush to get tasks completed efficiently, Mary had overlooked the volunteers' need for recognition, friendship, and socialization.

In a related vein, Mary's supervisor began hearing teasing remarks about her being isolated and overly concerned with paperwork. They joked about whether Mary was afraid to get out and meet the people. Mary wondered whether she had overemphasized the importance of getting a good plan at the expense of meeting community leaders. She also wondered if it was always going to be this difficult deciding whether to allocate her time to getting things done or satisfying the needs of people.

Questions
ع

1. Why do people volunteer to be on committees?

2. How do the needs of volunteers differ from the needs of paid staff? Since volunteers are not rewarded by a paycheck, what rewards do they receive for their work?

3. Was it wise for Mary to sacrifice proper introductions (people processes) to get a successful plan completed on time (goal achievement processes)?

4. What needs does a plan serve for the planner, for those who commission a plan, for the volunteers who develop the plan, and for the public? How does one decide whose needs take precedent?

CASE TWELVE

ₑₐ

The Politically Correct Candidate

As Joe pondered the chances of being promoted to Executive Director of Family and Children's Center (FCC), Inc., he considered, as he had numerous times in his career, whether his ethnicity would be a critical factor in whether or not he got the job, and, whether it would be used for or against him.

Growing up in the Southwest, Joe had experienced his share of prejudice and discrimination. The earliest incident he recalled was as a student in the fourth grade, when the Anglo teacher, angry at one of the students, turned to the class of brown faces and declared that they never would amount to more than the ditch diggers working outside the classroom. At the time, Joe was too young to catch the meaning of her prophecy. His favorite uncle was a ditch digger and was much admired in the neighborhood because he had a steady job and could afford to send his kids to the movies on Sunday.

It wasn't until Joe graduated from elementary school that he felt the full force of racism. He, along with the other students completing the seventh grade, were given the choice of either attending the "white" or the "Mexican" junior high school. Not wanting to expose Joe to the gangs and drugs of the southside school, his parents selected the Anglo junior high. What followed for Joe was two years of hell. There was, however, a happy ending. The hell consisted of constant ridicule by the white students of Joe's accent, and their total shunning of him from their social activities. The happy ending was due to one teacher, Mrs. Brick, who stayed after class to give Joe lessons in diction. Joe's (and Mrs. Brick's) proudest moment came

83

when he recited, in near-perfect English, the Gettysburg Address in her civics class a week before graduation.

Joe's next major encounter with discrimination occurred after he graduated from college. Armed with a degree in English Literature, he scrounged the corporate and governmental halls of employment opportunity only to learn that a BA held by a Mexican American, in his hometown, was not legal tender. The light company, where he applied for a job in the public relations department, offered him a job as a meter reader. The First National Bank would not hire him as a teller but would consider him for its custodial department. Others simply took his application and never called back. Joe arrived at the conclusion that being a Mexican American with an English degree was double jeopardy.

Ethnicity finally paid off, however. Joe was hired by the human services department of the county not because he knew anything about social work but purely on the basis of his being bilingual. He liked and excelled at the work, and got a scholarship to attend graduate school. Joe was pleased that the scholarship was not based on race but on scholarship — on his academic track record. In fact, after he enrolled and applied for additional assistance, he was told that he was ineligible because the only grant money available was for minorities, and the only minorities the university at that time recognized were Blacks and foreign students.

Joe's first promotion, upon returning from graduate school, was hotly debated by the Board of Directors of the human services agency. One of the questions raised by one board member was whether Joe could be impartial in providing services to members of his "own group." Another director questioned Joe's ability to represent the agency in public — "How will the folks out there respond to a Mexican?" Joe got the promotion but no others in that agency because the powers-that-be never felt "the folks out there" were ready for a social work administrator who happened to be Mexican American.

Eventually, ethnicity paid off again. Joe was hired by the Federal government in a high position in the Department of Health, Education, and Welfare. Unfortunately, he was the token in-house Chicano in the Children's Bureau. Of course, he had no responsibilities or authority, but was paraded by his bosses before protesting groups of Chicanos to indicate the bureau's sensitivity to their concerns.

After 1 year of servitude, Joe returned to the Southwest to head a private minority "parallel institution" — an agency designed to address culture-specific social needs of Mexican Americans. During those years, he no longer had to wonder whether his ethnicity was a factor in his work. He knew it was.

When funds for minority projects dried up, Joe moved back into the mainstream of social welfare services. He joined Family and Children's Center because they needed a bilingual social worker to serve a growing "Hispanic" population. As the demands for service from the Hispanic community grew, Joe developed and presented to the Executive Director a plan to establish a branch office in the Hispanic barrio of the community. Moreover, he wrote a grant proposal for its funding. The plan and proposal were presented to the Board, and the proposal, after board approval, was submitted to several foundations. The proposal was funded, and Joe became the Branch Director for Hispanic Affairs of the Family and Children's Center, Inc.

Two years later, the Executive Director of FCC announced her retirement. Before doing so, she had approached Joe about applying for the position. She had confidence in him and knew he could handle the job. Joe said he could, but wondered whether the mostly white, male, corporate-type board members were "ready for an Hispanic administrator." She said she wasn't sure, but that the agency was ready for Joe.

Together with other applicants for the position, Joe was scheduled for an employment interview. When his turn came, he was summoned into the agency's conference room by Betty, the Executive Secretary. Mr. Barnes, the President of the Board, started the process by welcoming Joe and briefly reviewing Joe's employment and educational history. When he finished, Jack Donohoe, the Vice-President, asked Joe how he felt about the growing number of "illegal Mexican aliens" coming north and depleting social agencies of scarce resources. Next, Sister Bonaventura, Board Secretary, asked Joe to account for the lack of interest on the part of Hispanic parents in their children's education. This was followed by a question by one other board member of whether Joe considered himself a Mexican American, a Chicano, or a Hispanic.

At that point, Joe stood up and said: "I came here prepared to talk about the agency's goals and objectives, about funding for the future, about unmet social need that the agency can address. I did not come to discuss international problems, the dynamics of Hispanic family life, or what I prefer to call myself. Take your pick. I can see that in the final analysis, in this state, and in this board room, a spic is a spic is a spic. Your questions convince me of one thing: Given the choice between being Executive Director of an agency that is concerned only with my race, and being a ditch digger, I'll choose the latter."

The next day, Joe was informed by Board President Barnes that he had unanimously been selected as the next Executive Director of Family and Children's Services, Inc.

Questions
ະ

1. How would you explain Joe's indignant response to the Board during the employment interview?

2. Why did FCC Board members, in the light of their comments during the interview, select Joe to the position of Executive Director?

3. What are the pros and cons of a social worker using his or her minority status as a means of career advancement?

4. If you were Joe, under the circumstances, would you have accepted the position of Executive Director of FCC? Why?

5. How has your own gender, race, and ethnicity affected your career?

CASE THIRTEEN

ε**a**

Who's the Boss?

One of Merle's first responsibilities after having been hired by the state child protection agency to direct one of its County Child Welfare Units was to fill a vacant child welfare worker position. After interviewing several applicants, Merle offered the position to Jim, a 21-year-old recent college graduate with a degree in English literature. Although Jim knew nothing about social work or child protective services, Merle selected him because of his relative maturity, his self-confidence, and his apparent compassion for others.

Under Merle's supervision, Jim soon distinguished himself as an effective beginning child welfare worker. He was encouraged by Merle, who had an MSW from Columbia University, and by her boss, Jerome, the Regional Child Welfare Director, to seek graduate education. With their help, Jim obtained a scholarship to one of the most prestigious schools of social work in the country. Upon graduation, he returned to the unit and was immediately promoted by Merle to Intake Supervisor in charge of five workers and one secretary. As supervisor, Jim demonstrated the ability to make sound decisions regarding the protection of children as well as the ability to be a supportive yet firm manager. By then, he and Merle had developed a very close professional relationship. Jim appreciated the fact that although 20 years his senior, Merle had never treated him maternalistically.

Two years after Jim's return from graduate school, Jerome announced his retirement as Regional Director. Merle was called into the state office. She returned with the State Director of Child Welfare Services, Pat. Pat and Merle met with Jim, and the next day called a staff meeting to let staff know that Merle had been promoted to Regional Director and Jim to Unit Director. Somehow, staff were not surprised by these developments. The news, however, was greeted with mixed feelings by some of the unit supervisors, most of whom had developed strong allegiances to Merle over the years and were not sure how they would feel having Jim as their boss. These reactions had been anticipated by Pat, Merle, and Jim, who were prepared to openly discuss them with staff.

At the beginning, unit supervisors continued to relate to Merle as their leader, and, as the Regional Director's office was in the same building as the Unit, they tended to seek her out for supervision or consultation. Patiently and deliberately, Merle helped her former supervisees to accept the transition and their new leader. In time, as supervisors got to know Jim as their supervisor, they began to transfer their allegiance from Merle to him.

The biggest problem resulting from the promotion was not with staff, however. The real resistance came from the County Child Welfare Board, a group of 15 civic leaders appointed by County Commissioners Court to oversee spending of county funds by the state unit. For years, they had worked with Merle and had developed a great deal of respect for her. Moreover, she and they traveled in the same social circles and had common sociopolitical connections. Jim, on the other hand, was a youngster with no social or political credentials. Although never outright hostile, the Board let Jim know in subtle ways that it would be difficult for him to fill Merle's shoes.

Ironically, one of the reasons Merle had decided to accept the regional post was that she was tired of handling the financial and political aspects of running the unit. She had always dreaded budget preparations and presentations, and for that duty had relied heavily on the treasurer of the board. (Needless to say, the Treasurer was not too pleased when Jim proved capable of preparing and presenting the budget all by himself.) As Regional Director, Merle would have no budget worries. Her staff of two regional licensing and two regional adoption workers were all paid directly by state office. They were all housed in space provided by the local unit, which also supplied equipment and supplies.

As Regional Director, Merle's primary duties were to provide protective services in all counties which were "uncovered," i.e., did not have a county child welfare agency. In her five-county farming and ranching region, only one county had a unit. All adoption and

child-care licensing applications were handled by the regional adoption and licensing staff. Another responsibility was to encourage
commissioners' courts in the various uncovered counties to establish local county child welfare offices.

Whereas during Jerome's tenure the region had been a rather
placid environment involving one, perhaps two, child abuse and
neglect reports per month, complaints began to increase soon after
Merle's promotion. Consequently, she found herself traveling in the
vast, sparsely inhabited region much more than she had anticipated.
Not only that, the only way to get the rural communities in a region
about the size of Maine was by automobile. The increase in abuse
and neglect reports, and the pressure put on commissioners by residents to establish local units kept Merle on the road almost constantly. After a year of almost incessant travel, she requested to
return to her job as director of the local unit. Before doing so, however, Merle had approached Jim about becoming Regional Director.
Although Jim was happy in his post as Unit Director, the potential
raise in salary involved proved to be a big inducement in this agree-
ing to switch jobs with Merle. The state office approved the plan and
the reversal of roles was announced: Jim would become Merle's boss.

The board welcomed the news — especially the Board Treasurer. Supervisors who knew Merle were not displeased by the
switch, since they found both her and Jim's leadership styles very
similar. Everything seemed to go smoothly until a vacancy occurred
in the secretarial staff of the unit. Merle asked Jim's approval to
promote JoAnn to unit secretary, a position vacated by Patsy, who
had been both Merle's and Jim's secretary. Before Merle's return to
the unit, Jim had "promised" the position to Millie if Patsy ever left.
He had discussed this with Merle, then Regional Director and
responsible for approving all unit promotions, and she had con-
curred. As Unit Supervisor, however, she felt that she could work
better with JoAnn. Jim approved Merle's recommendation and
JoAnn was promoted. Millie, expecting the promotion, quit upon
learning of JoAnn's selection, and two other secretaries threatened
to leave over Jim's "double-crossing" Millie. Jim felt angry at himself for having let Merle sway him from his original selection of
Millie. For the first time in their long association, Jim felt resentment toward his old boss — an old boss who was now, at least on
paper, his subordinate.

This incident was followed by several other, though minor, ones
in which Merle questioned Jim's administrative decisions and tried

to modify them. The final blow to the relationship happened when Merle, in front of staff, criticized Jim for his arrangement of new furniture in the reception room. Frustrated, Jim shouted, addressing Merle by her last name, "Mrs. Addison, when, if ever, will you let me be the boss?" The look of shock on Merle's face genuinely frightened Jim, who walked away and shut himself in his office for the rest of the morning.

That evening, Merle's husband called Jim to say that Merle had been taken to the hospital by ambulance after she came home and apparently suffered a heart attack. Next morning, Jim visited Merle in the hospital. She assured him that it had been a mild attack, and rejected Jim's attribution of it to their spat over the furniture. Merle was released from the hospital and returned to work the following week. Jim submitted his resignation as Regional Director the following month.

Questions
ra.

1. Promotions from within can produce serious relationship problems within organizations. Critically analyze the decision to have Jim and Merle reverse supervisory roles.

2. As a supervisee, what steps could Merle have taken to facilitate the transition?

3. As a supervisor, what steps could Jim have taken to prevent the final confrontation?

4. Discuss the pros and cons of Jim's resignation.

5. Have you ever worked in an organization where personal friendships between supervisor and staff impacted on organizational functioning? Cite the ethical and organizational pitfalls of such relationships.

CASE FOURTEEN

⁊⁊

New Directions

New Directions is a 24-hour residential group home for disturbed adolescents. The Director of the agency is Denise Johnson, who has been in that position for 10 years. Ms. Johnson is very well known in the social work community due to her activism, fundraising ability, and success at creating visibility for her agency. Ms. Johnson professes to embody a democratic, participative style of leadership. For example, she encourages employees to make suggestions at the weekly staff meetings and often employs a problem-solving method with her staff that involves "brainstorming" and consensus building. Nevertheless, she typically ignores her staff's opinions and makes her own decisions. After the initial consensus has been reached, she often makes and implements a contradictory decision without conferring with staff members. In fact, staff actually play a minor role in decision-making.

Furthermore, Ms. Johnson's main approach to achieving her own goals within the agency is to maintain complete control over almost every aspect of agency operations, from the supervision of custodial staff, clerical staff, and direct care workers to the selection of board members and coordination of board meetings. Ms. Johnson rarely delegates decision-making responsibilities to others. In those rare instances that she does delegate, she is constantly questioning and second-guessing the decision that has been made. In addition to these administrative duties, she likes to keep in contact with clients, so she conducts group therapy once a week for residents.

By controlling every aspect of agency operations, Ms. Johnson makes herself appear indispensable to the agency. Furthermore, on the whole, board members are long-time associates of the Executive Director and have been hand-picked by her. She chooses board members based on their perceived loyalty to her and then consults with the President of the Board to get the nomination approved. The board members are largely shielded from activities in the agency and have no perspective on the agency other than that of the Director's. She thus has the almost total and complete support of the Board of Directors. Also, staff are barred from communicating with the Board. Thus Ms. Johnson is able to achieve policy and personnel decisions quickly as she really does not have to consult with anyone beside a small group of the board that she calls her "kitchen cabinet".

There is only one board member who occasionally opposes an action taken by Ms. Johnson. This board member usually has little or no support from other board members. When Mr. Tuttle raises an issue or concern about some decision of Ms. Johnson's, he is often met by embarrassed silence by the rest of the Board. The President asks Ms. Johnson to explain her position, and most board members listen intently or nod in agreement as she speaks. The issue is then dropped.

The morale of the staff at the agency is low since staff are often intimidated by the Director, feel that their suggestions go unheeded, and that there is little opportunity for them to grow in their positions. Staff have become more and more distrustful of Ms. Johnson and are hesitant to express concerns and opinions about agency matters. In addition, her management style creates an atmosphere of mistrust among the staff as she constantly thinks of ways to "divide and conquer," to reward them for loyalty to her, and discourage group cohesion. All of this has led to high staff turnover.

When staff leave, it is often difficult to find replacements. Months go by and the remaining staff becomes overburdened by the additional work. As vacancies are not filled, the agency often operates with the minimum number of staff required by law for group homes. In addition, the Assistant Director of the agency resigned last year due to unresolved differences with the Director regarding proper management of the agency. The position has not been filled because the Director is more concerned with loyalty than competence, indeed feels threatened by competent staff, and therefore can not find anyone she trusts enough to fill the position of Assistant Director. Other positions are often filled by newly degreed bachelor's level staff as they are less expensive, and usually do not have the experience or sophistication to oppose Ms. Johnson.

Yet, Ms. Johnson is able to convince her board that she is doing everything she can to attract and retain the most qualified people. She often diverts them from the internal problems in the agency by real and conjured external threats to the agency in the form of funding cuts, budget problems, threatened lawsuits by parents, and slights to her reputation and by implication, that of the agency. She involves them in fundraising and community activities that, while beneficial to the agency, deflect their attention from the management problems of the agency.

No person can be several places at once, and Ms. Johnson often spends her time on minutiae, micromanaging the agency because there is no one else willing or able to take responsibility for anything not approved by her. This situation has been created by her, yet she often feels weighed down by all her work. She frequently complains about the hours, even weekends, that she spends on the job.

The last straw for many staff involved a client who was about to be discharged. At a case meeting in which a decision had to be made regarding the discharge and placement of a 17-year-old female resident, Ms. Johnson asked for input regarding this decision. The staff, noting the remarkable progress the resident had made in this structured environment over the previous 18 months, agreed that this resident should be discharged the following month. She was to complete her GED and several other treatment goals, and be placed in foster care. Ms. Johnson said that she would go along with the staff consensus. Yet, 2 days later, without consulting the staff, she discharged the patient prematurely, and instead of placing her in foster care, allowed her to go into independent living in the home of a 21-year-old relative. Several staff members expressed their disappointment at her lack of commitment to the original group consensus and their disapproval of her decision. Ms. Johnson responded that she was the Executive Director and had final responsibility for determining what is in the best interest of the agency's clients. Several staff believed that she had really made the decision because of pressure from a relative of the client who had promised a large donation to the home. They were furious. Some of them called a surreptitious meeting of the staff to decide whether they should go to the board with their complaints. Others question the value of the effort, since they may lose their jobs.

Questions

ҙ

1. How would you characterize Ms. Johnson's leadership style?

2. What are some positive aspects of a leadership style such as this?

3. What are some negative aspects of this style?

4. How would you describe your own leadership style?

5. How would you deal with this situation if you were:
   A. a staff member?
   B. the lone dissenting member of the Board?

CASE FIFTEEN

ða

Whose Values: The Politics of Planning

Jennifer was upset. Just two months before, she thought she would be promoted to Executive Director. Now, her only choice seemed to be to quit her job.

It all started 6 months before when she was asked to staff a committee charged with planning for community based services for the mental health center where she worked. She had been pushing the center's executive director to set up community programs, which she felt educated and empowered clients, and focused on prevention rather than treatment. The agency, she felt, was traditionally oriented with an individualistic model of mental health treatment. While this traditional model fit the conservative, middle-class community it served, Jennifer felt that it was inappropriate for addressing the problems of the disadvantaged and of youth. Jennifer was chosen to staff the planning committee because of her ideas about community support services. She had researched advocacy, empowerment, and prevention in graduate school, and finally had the opportunity to implement her ideas.

Jennifer had selected a 12-member planning committee based on their willingness to work and their potential to attract funds. The committee was composed of several service providers and concerned citizens. The committee worked well together, and easily agreed on the mission statement and guiding principles. Based on their needs assessment, they had developed an implementation strategy, and wrote a grant to obtain funding for the top priority needs. The grant was to fund an agency that used youth and elderly volunteers to

95

provide support and education to low-income, at-risk citizens. The agency would also operate a client-managed halfway house which would provide self-help events for the community. While advocacy was a key component of all services, it had not been explicitly stated in the grant in order to not antagonize the conservative foundation from which funds were sought.

To insure that the new program would receive local support, the planning committee recommended that the county, city, school district, and local industry appoint 75% of the board. The remaining board members were to be members of the planning committee. The mental health center was to provide a full-time staff person to help the board for the first six months.

The board was appointed when the proposal received three-year funding from the foundation. While the board was more conservative and politically motivated than Jennifer had hoped, she thought that this conservative nature might insure acceptance and future funding. Jennifer had privately expressed interest in becoming the executive director of this new agency to her boss and to some planning committee members. This promotion was supported by everyone she talked to. That was, until the first meeting of the new board.

The Mayor had appointed a high school football coach as the city's representative. The coach was authoritarian with students, but well liked by parents. He was very conservative politically and had been involved with the mayor's campaign. The coach was never able to develop a winning football team and the rumor was that his contract had not been renewed. Other board members included the school board president and a nurse from the county hospital. To Jennifer's dismay, the coach was elected chair of the board at its first meeting.

At the board's second meeting, Jennifer's plans seemed to crumble. The whole philosophy of the program was ignored, especially the self-help, advocacy, and empowerment focus. What the board seemed to understand were buildings and the traditional model of treatment. When board members from the original planning committee tactfully raised several issues about treatment philosophy, the coach ignored their concerns. After several unsuccessful tries at bringing up issues, they remained silent.

Jennifer could not hold her frustration any longer. She asked for the floor and then briefly discussed the long planning process, the needs assessment, and the philosophy behind the agency. The coach made a joking but blunt remark that the role of paid staff was not to push their philosophy, but to help the new board implement whatever programs the board developed. He indicated that the board was responsible for the new agency, and was not bound by the details of the plan or the grant.

Jennifer's worst suspicions were realized as the board discussed the qualifications of the agency's Executive Director. The qualifications stressed project management and working with people. Nevertheless, a human service degree and human service experience were not mentioned. As the meeting ended, the coach indicated that he might apply for the job. Several board members indicated that they thought he would make a good Executive Director.

Jennifer felt she could no longer staff the board which ignored the ideas for which she had worked so hard. No one else in her Mental Health Center, however, was interested in the new agency. Her request to be replaced might anger her boss and colleagues, who might think she welcomed the prestige of the planning position, but quit when her feelings and personal interests were hurt. Could she really continue to staff the board? Could she work closely with the coach if the coach became the Executive Director? Could she work hard to make the very traditional program envisioned by the coach successful?

Jennifer had a decision to make. But what criteria could she use? The decision involved her emotions, her professional philosophy, and her career. Could she be objective? Why had graduate school or other professional training not prepared her to make tough decisions like this one?

Questions

ta

1. To what degree is it appropriate for Jennifer to promote her own candidacy for the position of Executive Director? For the coach to do so?

2. Was it unethical or unprofessional for Jennifer to deemphasize advocacy in the grant application?

3. Is the role of paid committee staff to push the philosophy they feel is best, or is it only to carry out the wishes of the

committee, even though they do not agree philosophically with those wishes?

4. Was the coach any different from Jennifer in pushing his philosophy?

5. What next steps would you suggest Jennifer take?

CASE SIXTEEN

ને

A Problem Within

Mike is a professionally trained and experienced counselor, but he has never confronted this situation before. Solving other people's problems is easy. Solving one so close to home involves complications that make Mike unsure of what to do.

The problem surfaced at a workshop on the alcoholic-personality. The behavior patterns of an alcohol dependent employee were listed: mid to late forties, hardworking, increased absences from work or work in isolation, deteriorating performance at times, mood swings, irritability, and denial. The workshop leader asked participants to try to visualize someone who fit the symptoms. Mike shut his eyes and relaxed. Suddenly, he broke into a cold sweat when the Executive Director popped into his mind. The symptoms fit, but could it be true?

Mike is Director of Counseling in a medium sized mental health center. He had risen through the ranks from counselor to supervisor and program director. He and the five other Program Directors, who were in their mid-thirties to mid-forties, reported directly to the Executive Director, who is 47 years old. The management style in the agency is competitive. Program Directors compete with each other, and all aspire to become an Executive Director.

Mike wondered what he should do. The first alternative was to confront the situation head on. Could he confront his boss about such a sensitive issue? He knew that confrontation was often futile, due to the strong denial associated with alcoholism. Wouldn't confrontation make matters worse?

Another alternative was to document the alcoholic behavior pattern and to use this documentation when confronting the executive. Did a pattern exist? The Program Directors and the Executive Director often drank socially at conferences and after work on Friday afternoons. Recently, the executive seemed to drink more during their Friday afternoon "attitude adjustment periods." At least three counselors mentioned that they smelled alcohol on the Executive Director's breath during the day. One suggested jokingly not to ask for a raise before the executive had his afternoon break. This possible drinking could be explained, however, because the executive was having marital problems.

Ah ha, home problems, another symptom? Mike was wondering whether he was reading too much into the situation. He remembered his first abnormal psychology class. When reading about each abnormal behavior pattern, he quickly recognized someone he knew. The symptoms seemed to fit his friends and relatives, who were obviously not mentally ill. Was he doing the same in this situation?

Another alternative in helping the alcoholic employee was to educate the existing support network, and use it to confront and guide the employee. But, how could he build the support network without looking as if he were starting rumors? Could he approach board members without jeopardizing the executive's job, or without appearing to be ousting the executive to become executive himself? Everyone knew that he and the other Program Directors aspired to be the Executive Director of an agency. Would the board not see his approach as an attempt to plant suspicions and maybe as a mutiny? Would some of the other Program Directors use a weakened executive to further their personal ambitions?

What about talking to the executive's wife? But wouldn't she be afraid of the executive losing his job? Denial might even be stronger for her as she had put her career on hold to raise her family. Agency policies allowed 3 months paid leave for physical problems, but Mike was unsure whether the agency's insurance carrier considered alcoholism a physical or psychological problem. He felt uneasy asking for clarification now.

Finally, he might consult other agencies, such as an Employee Assistance Program or the Council on Alcoholism. Most agencies knew Mike, however, and recognized his voice. By asking for advice, he could start a rumor. Wouldn't a rumor make the situation worse, particularly if his boss really had a problem?

What about doing nothing? Would he violate professional ethics by remaining silent when he suspected that someone needed help? Was he ruling out alternatives based on self preservation rather than ethical behavior? Was his fear of confrontation, and of jeopardizing his career, biasing his approach to the problem? Should he wait until the problem became worse, and thus more obvious? He knew that early treatment dramatically increases the chances of recovery. By doing nothing, would he increase the Executive Director's problems? Would it increase the chances of a divorce and thereby deprive the Executive Director of a support network vital to recovery?

Mike decided he needed more facts before acting. He would scan the literature to find additional insights and solutions. He would begin to chart patterns in the Executive Director's behavior, and listen for clues among colleagues and board members. He would note periodic absences from work or isolated periods from staff where drinking by the executive could occur. He would observe the executive for the subtle changes associated with problem drinking.

While Mike had reached a decision, he felt uneasy. He was unsure of whether he was acting responsibly or irresponsibly.

Questions

1. Was Mike acting responsibly?

2. Can professional ethics offer any guidance to Mike?

3. Do you agree with Mike's reasoning as he ruled out each alternative for solving the problem? If not, what reasoning do you not agree with?

4. What would you do in the same situation?

5. Are other details needed about this case before you could give advice? If so, what are they?

6. What about Mike going to his boss to talk privately about his concerns? What about privately talking to the boss's wife?

7. In considering the problem of alcoholism, must Mike only consider job-related behavior and performance, or can he consider behavior off the job?

CASE SEVENTEEN

ૐ

A Sexual Harassment Complaint

John Simmons is the Program Director of an adoption program run by the State Department of Human Services. There are six such regional adoption programs around the state. This program tries to find permanent placements for infants and children whose parents have relinquished parental rights. There are ten workers in John's unit. Most workers are at the same governmental rank, although some have seniority based on years of service. As state employees, all human service workers are covered by a binding union contract that specifies conditions of employment, salaries, benefits, and so forth.

One morning, one of John's workers, Rita Rutledge, stormed into his office.

"You have got to do something about Dan," she said furiously. "And if you don't, I'm going to take action!" she threatened ominously.

John stood up and came out from behind his desk.

"Calm down, Rita," he said soothingly. "Sit down and tell me what's happened."

"Dan is a sexist, and he's sexually harassing me!"

John thought of Dan Clarke, an Adoption Specialist who had been with his unit for 4 years. He seemed quiet and unassuming; John could not imagine him sexually harassing anyone. John knew that Dan and Rita were both married and seemed to relate well to their coworkers. He had noticed no unusual dynamic between them.

John thought of the work culture in his office and the type of work climate he had tried to foster. Working in human services with children was very stressful, many of the children came from abused backgrounds and had multiple physical and/or emotional handicaps. The workers were constantly beating the bushes, searching for suitable families who would nurture these children. They also had to deal with the traumatic aftermaths of failed matches, those instances when potential families returned children to the agency because of their inability to cope with the child. Because of the stress they were under, and the commitment they felt to their agency's mission, there was a closeness and sense of common purpose among the workers in the unit. There was an *esprit de corps* in the unit and everyone pitched in to help if there was an emergency.

There were seven women and three men in the unit. There was much joking and kidding around among whomever was working on the "floor." All of the workers in the unit worked at desks lined up in rows, the adoption unit was separated from other programs by simple movable six-foot partitions. If Dan had done anything, surely everyone in the unit had seen it.

"What has Dan done to you?" asked John.

"It all started last year at the office Christmas party," began Rita. "Dan put his arm around me when we were singing Christmas songs. I didn't like it, but I didn't say anything. I just gradually moved away from him. Ever since then he has smiled at me in a suggestive manner and he is constantly asking me out to have a drink with him. It is getting on my nerves."

"Has he ever touched you since that time?"

"No."

"Has he ever said anything of a sexual nature to you?"

"No."

"What did you mean when you said he smiled at you in a suggestive manner? Does he look at your body or make any sort of gestures?"

"No, it's just that his smile is more of a leer."

"Have you told him that you don't want to have a drink with him?"

"More than once," replied Rita, "but he keeps insisting. I feel very uncomfortable around him, I won't be alone with him. Who knows what he would do?"

This displeased John greatly, as a small unit such as his could ill afford such dissension among the caseworkers. In-fighting within the unit could undermine the team spirit he had tried so hard to build.

"Let me talk to Dan and see what he has to say, then I'll get back to you, okay?"

"Well, alright, but I'm telling you John, something better be done about this, or I'm going to see an attorney."

Later that day, John called Dan to his office and asked him about his relationship with Rita.

"Dan, Rita came in here very angry today to complain that you were bothering her. What's going on?"

"Why should she be angry with me? I haven't done anything to her," answered Dan with a quizzical look on his face. "If anything, I have always been helpful to her."

"Have you asked her out for drinks?"

"Yes, but you know lots of people from the office go out once in a while for a drink. It's a way to unwind and get stuff off your chest. What's the big deal?"

"Have you asked her more than once?"

"Yes, because when she was asked she would say something like 'another time' or 'later'. If she didn't want to go, why didn't she just say no? She knew I was just being friendly."

"What happened at the Christmas party last year," asked John.

"Nothing happened at the Christmas party."

"Did you touch Rita?"

"Did I touch her?" Dan stopped to think. "I guess I might have put my arm around her when everyone was singing, but I was just being friendly. Anyway, I have never touched her any other time before or since, so what is she making a big deal about this now for?"

"Well, said John, "she's feeling harassed and says she's afraid to be alone with you in the same room."

Dan stood up. "You know what I think?" he exploded, "I think something else is going on here and you're playing right into it whether you know it or not! You know damn well that Rita and I both took the civil service exam for promotion to Caseworker II. I think she's trying to discredit me so she can get the job. You know there's only one position available. I'm not going to let her get away with this. I'm calling my attorney!" he yelled as he turned and walked out.

John sat at his desk thinking about his next course of action. He was surprised at the vehemence and anger on both sides and wondered if mediation was possible. He knew very little about the legal issues regarding sexual harassment. He was not even too certain about departmental policies regarding it. He vaguely remembered an afternoon workshop about it a year or two ago that all supervisors were required to attend. He hadn't paid much attention because he never thought it would happen in his unit. And he was only vaguely aware of a recent Supreme Court decision that said a key determining factor in harassment is what a reasonable person of the same sex as the complainant considers harassment.

He turned to the shelf near his desk where his policies and procedures manual was located. He opened to the section entitled "Sexual Harassment" and began to read:

"Sexual harassment of employees or clients is a form of sex discrimination prohibited by law. The Department of Human Services has both informal and formal procedures for resolving complaints.

In differentiating between actions that constitute sexual harassment and those that establish a strictly personal, social relationship without discriminatory effects, the agency applies the following criteria:

Unwelcome sexual advances, requests for sexual favors, and other verbal or physical conduct of a sexual nature constitute sexual harassment when:

1. submission to such conduct is made, explicitly or implicitly, a term or condition of an individual's employment;

2. submission or rejection of such conduct is used as the basis for decisions affecting an individual's employment status; or

3. such conduct has the purpose or effect of unreasonably interfering with an individual's work performance or creating an intimidating, hostile, or offensive work environment.

Persons who wish to file a formal complaint should contact the Director, Office of Affirmative Action/Equal Opportunity, at the state capital."

Questions
ᨑ

1. What should John do?

2. What responsibilities do organizations and supervisors have in preventing harassment in the workplace?

3. What should be some key components of an anti-harassment policy?

CASE EIGHTEEN

&

Inertia on the Board

Senior Citizens of Metro County has been in existence for over 25 years. Its goals are to help older adults improve the quality of their lives and maintain their dignity and self-esteem. As with most human service agencies, the Board is legally responsible for the policies and decisions made by the agency. The Board's function is to establish goals, develop policies and procedures, and oversee the fiduciary responsibility of the agency. It delegates the day-to-day operations of the agency to the Executive Director, Loretta Thomas.

Years ago, the Board developed a Board Manual. Major duties of the Board are listed as:

1. To manage the business and property of the agency.

2. To adopt and review policies that govern the operating procedures of the agency.

3. To make final decisions on overall policies that govern the scope of the agency's programs and that enable the agency to reach its goals.

4. To approve personnel policies and assure that they are kept current with standards of good practice.

5. To establish, approve, and control the agency budget and financial plan.

6. To help develop sound agency/community relationships.

7. To represent the agency in community affairs.

8. To concern itself with the needs of senior citizens of the community.

The Board consists of 34 members, although its by-laws state that a maximum of forty are allowed. Of the members currently serving, 21 are male, and 11 are female. Most of the clients served by the agency are elderly women. That the client base is primarily women is attributed to two factors: 1, women live longer than men; 2, women tend to utilize social services more than men. The members of the board range in age from 46 to 78. The majority are white and represent all socioeconomic levels, although they tend to be clustered in the upper-middle class. Board member occupations include one banker, one professor, some business owners, management level people from some of the companies in the area, ministers, housewives, and a number of retired people. In fact, more than three-quarters of the Board is made up of retired people.

The officers of the Board include a president, vice-president, recording secretary, and treasurer. The nominating committee presents names of persons to be considered to fill board vacancies, and additional nominations can be submitted by other Board members. There is no set term for members. Vacancies are usually filled after a member stops coming to meetings.

The people who sit on the nominating committee are the most powerful and influential as they select the names of persons to be presented to the board for consideration. There is no active recruitment program for new members, and no public announcement is made when a vacancy arises. New members are nominated because someone on the nominating committee knows them. Occasionally, existing Board members may recruit someone from outside their social circle to be on the Board; but once recruited, these "outsiders" gradually stop coming to meetings. Also, because of the frequency and time of the meetings, it is very difficult to recruit working people for the Board. In addition, as very little of substance ever takes place at the meetings, it is difficult to sustain the interest and enthusiasm of new members. Therefore, what remains is the same small group of people who have been coming to the meetings for the last 10 years or more.

The Board meets monthly, for 2 to 3 hours in the afternoon, in a conference room at the agency. When the board members are there, the agency's work virtually comes to a stop as the Board members are constantly bothering staff to use the copy machine or the telephones, and sit, talking loudly, in the waiting room.

Loretta Thomas has become increasingly frustrated by the Board and its inaction. She has attended meeting after meeting where nothing ever seems to be accomplished. Furthermore, it is very time-consuming for her to prepare for these meetings, as she is constantly being asked for reports at the meetings. During her presentations, there seems to be little interest, and nothing is done with the reports. She realizes that the Board and its meetings serve many different social and emotional needs of the members, while the needs of the agency go unmet. She recognizes that the Board is run and controlled by a small clique of people who are self-perpetuating in the officer posts and thus control the agenda of the board.

Often, only about five or six members regularly show up, not enough for a quorum, but they continue to meet even though no formal business can be transacted. The few newer members have come to complain to her about the board being a "social club." Knowing she has some allies on the Board who want to move for change, she decides she has to do something to help the agency.

Loretta believes that one important function of a Board is fundraising. The agency staff need critical help in this area as the agency's United Way allocation has been cut due to a downturn in the economy. In addition, federal spending cuts have severely affected the hot meals program run by the agency. She thinks the board ought to recruit members with expertise in the areas of marketing and fundraising. But every time she tries to bring up the subject with the Board, she is met with murmurs of support and little else.

Loretta wants to do something to get new "blood" on the Board. She believes that one diplomatic way to do this is to work with Board members on revising the by-laws. If she can get them to agree to term limits for service she can get some of the "old guard" off the board. She talks to one of the newer members who had previously complained to her, Stan Edwards, and he agrees to work with her in redirecting the board. He is respected by the other members of the board, although he is not one of the "insiders." Nevertheless, he is energetic and very interested in the activities offered to seniors as his mother has just started attending the agency's senior center.

At the next Board meeting, when Loretta is discussing the up-coming United Way management audit, Stan brings up the subject of the board's functions. He says that preparing for the audit is the perfect opportunity for the agency and the Board to review its mission and goals and how they are reflected in the by-laws. The other members agree and form a subcommittee chaired by Stan to review the by-laws.

After some months the by-laws are reviewed and revisions made. One of the new provisions is for 3-year terms for all members, renewable once. The revised by-laws are presented to the Board and unanimously approved. Initially, the existing Board members' terms are supposed to be randomly assigned so that one-third of the board will have a 1-year term, one-third a 2-year term, and one-third a 3-year term. That way one-third of the Board rotates off every year.

Loretta waits for the President to assign terms to all the members. Months pass and nothing happens. When Loretta asks why the members have not been assigned their terms, the President indicates that not enough members have been present at meetings for him to do this. She asks why he just doesn't assign the terms since they are supposed to be random assignments in any case. He just shrugs his shoulders.

Questions

1. What should be the role and function of a Board of Directors?

2. What are some components of a good Board Manual?

3. What types of training should be given new Board members?

4. What is the responsibility of staff vis-a-vis their Board?

5. What should Loretta do now about her Board?

CASE NINETEEN

ᘒ

The Price of Serving

When Marjie Wright was asked by her Junior League colleague and old college chum, Sarah Hill, to join the Board of Directors of Hope and Dignity, a newly incorporated shelter for battered women in Bay City, Marjie had mixed feelings about getting involved. She had heard stories and read newspaper accounts about the shelter and its "charismatic" (as one reporter described her) director, Felice Moody. Felice had turned her spacious home into a refuge for battered women soon after the death of her husband, M. S. ("Mouse") Moody, owner of Bay City's largest pest-control business. Marjie was also aware of the rumors floating about town that the health and zoning departments had cited Hope and Dignity for serious city code infractions, and that Felice had turned to Sarah, one of Bay City's most prestigious lawyers, for legal counsel. Marjie was especially concerned about news accounts of lack of policies and procedures regarding the management of the shelter. It was reported that no record of financial and in-kind contributions made to the shelter by individuals and businesses was kept. Nor were there any case records regarding clients served. All in all, it seemed like a pretty disorganized situation.

Why was Sarah asking Marjie to get involved in such a shaky organization?

For several reasons, Sarah explained. Number one, there was a need for such an agency in Bay City; the nearest other shelter was 60 miles away. Number two, Felice, an arts major with no managerial training or experience, needed all the help she could get to put the agency on its proper footing. Number three, Marjie had the managerial expertise and board experience to help the other new board members (none of whom had ever served on the board of a social service agency) make the decisions and provide the direction necessary to ensure the survival and success of Hope and Dignity.

Sarah's role had thus far been to help the agency develop its bylaws and obtain its charter as a non-profit corporation. She was in the process of helping Hope and Dignity obtain its 501(C) (3) designation from the Internal Revenue Service, and had agreed to serve as the agency's paid legal counsel. As such, she was ineligible to serve on the board. She had, nevertheless, agreed to help Felice recruit additional board members, and she could think of no one in the community better qualified than Marjie Wright, BBA, MSW, board member of Bay City Charities, Bay City YWCA, and Executive Director of the Bay City Child Care Association.

Reluctantly, Marjie agreed to join the board.

The first meeting of the newly constituted Board of Directors of Hope and Dignity, Inc., was held in what had been the Moody House library, now converted into a conference room dominated by a large oval table ringed by twelve leather high-back chairs, each occupied by a new board member. At the head of the table sat Felice, who, after introducing each board member, began talking about her hopes and dreams for the shelter. She appealed to the board members to work with her toward meeting the needs of the women who come to shelter. When she finished, Marjie complimented her on her dedication and commitment to the cause of battered women. She added that she felt sure all of the twelve board members shared her concerns, as demonstrated by their presence at the meeting. She wondered, however, what the purpose of this meeting was. All she had received was a notice announcing the time and place of the meeting. There had been no agenda enclosed and none was distributed at the meeting. It would help, she stated, if each director had a copy of the bylaws and started thinking about nominating officers and appointing committees.

Felice responded that those formalities would be attended to in time, but that she didn't want the board to be overly concerned about such matters and the "bureaucratic red tape" that accompanied them. It was her job to take care of the details. The board's role was to look at the "broad picture." As founder and director of Hope and Dignity, and as its sole source of financial support, Felice let the board know in no uncertain terms that she was in charge and that the board was there merely to fulfill non-profit corporate requirements. On that note, Felice suggested that the board break for coffee.

During the break it became obvious to Marjie that the other board members were either close friends or relatives of Felice, or former shelter clients. None seemed concerned about the role that Felice had cast them into; all appeared content with letting her "run the show." "It's her home and her money," one declared. "Not only that, she's a wonderful person and we all love and trust her," added another.

After the break, Felice announced that her sister, one of the new board members, had agreed to serve as president and that as president she would be appointing the other officers. All but Marjie joined in applauding the decision.

Next day, Marjie dictated a letter of resignation from the Board of Hope and Dignity, citing as her reason a concern that the board was not mindful of its legal and fiduciary responsibilities to the corporation. She sent a copy to her friend Sarah.

Three months later, Marjie read in the local newspaper that a man had gone to the shelter and physically attacked his wife, who had left him to seek refuge two weeks earlier. It was being alleged that a shelter employee had allowed the man to enter the home when he posed as a repairman. The woman required hospitalization and the man was incarcerated.

Some time after her recovery, the client sued the shelter, its director, and each of the members of the board for negligence in protecting her from her husband. Since Marjie was listed as a board member on the shelter's letterhead and there were no minutes or written agency record of her resignation prior to the incident, she was also sued, along with the other directors. Marjie hired a lawyer, who during the legal proceedings, was able to establish, primarily through the introduction of a copy of her letter of resignation, that Marjie was not a member of the corporation during the time the client was admitted to or injured in the shelter. The suit against her was dismissed. Even so, it cost Marjie $3,000 in legal fees and court costs to extricate herself from the proceedings.

Hope and Dignity, its Director, Felice, and its Board members were not as fortunate. They were found guilty of negligence in the operation of the corporation and were ordered to pay the client $300,000. Ironically, 2 weeks after the settlement, the client and her husband reconciled and moved to Kansas.

Questions

ใช

1. Discuss the role of the board of directors vis-à-vis the administrator and staff of the nonprofit social service agency.

2. Who should serve on a board, and how should members be chosen?

3. What is a 501 (c)(3) designation from the Internal Revenue Service?

4. What is meant by the "fiduciary and legal" responsibilities of the board of directors of a nonprofit corporation?

5. What steps could the Board members have taken to protect themselves and the agency from this situation?

CASE TWENTY

ȥ

"Creative" Grant Writing for Survival

Addictions ReCovery Corporation (ARCC) has to get a grant or lay off staff and possibly close down. ARCC operates three therapeutic self-help, halfway houses for recovering addicts. ARCC's 15 staff provide a therapeutic environment where recovering addicts receive interpersonal counseling, group support, and training on self-esteem and job skills.

ARCC was started by a large 5-year local foundation grant in response to the community's discovery that it had a crack cocaine problem. The grant was scheduled to end in 4 months. Initially, many resources were mobilized to prevent and rehabilitate addicts. Currently, however, many citizens view drug addiction as a familiar, almost unsolvable, urban problem. Moreover, treatment is "out of fashion" with most funding sources. Punitive approaches are being stressed along with short-term treatment based on the medical model. Funding sources are reluctant to commit scarce resources to long-term programs serving high-risk clients who often have committed criminal acts to fund their habit.

The original Executive Director moved on to a bigger agency in another state early in the fourth year of grant funding. He was seen by colleagues as having developed and operated an "acceptable" program. He had not developed a strong Board of Directors, nor prepared the agency for the end of the 5-year foundation grant. He had assured the board that another large foundation grant could be obtained, but suggested that ARCC should wait until 6 months before the present grant expired to apply for a new grant. The Board welcomed this approach, because it was positive and involved little extra work.

When Lori became the Executive Director she soon discovered the lack of long-term planning and board development. Since her first board meeting, Lori has tried to clarify that funding is not as available as in the past. Nevertheless, the board thinks that Lori can easily find continuation funding and dismisses her concern as lack of experience as an Executive Director. They were shocked when both the United Way and the original foundation turned down their application. They are finally beginning to understand that the program might not be able to survive in its present form. The Board does not know what to do and Lori cannot replace any Board members with others who have expertise in planning and fundraising until the next annual board meeting. Volunteers.

Lori only knows of a few sources of funds, and she has little hope of obtaining foundation funding. Foundations are reluctant to pick up programs started by another foundation that have failed to survive on their own. She has other ideas about solutions. The most promising options involve two new Federal programs. One new Federal program, which is based on the medical model, provides 30-day detoxification, intensive treatment, and referral to existing agencies for follow-up. Most of Lori's staff, however, are recovering addicts or counselors who have little faith in this medically oriented, short-term approach to treatment. The other Federal program is through the criminal justice system. It funds 15-day detoxification services to prisoners serving time for addiction-related offenses. Lori's staff have less enthusiasm for this model of treatment. Morale is low and many are looking for jobs in related agencies.

Lori has a decision to make. She can continue to uphold the ARCC's mission and therapeutic philosophy and begin the risky task of fundraising to keep current programs operating. She feels this would mean closing at least one or possibly two of the three half-way houses and laying off staff. The other options involve changing the treatment philosophy of the agency. She can attempt to persuade the board to re-orient ARCC's mission and philosophy toward either the medical model or the criminal justice model and write the appropriate Federal grant. Or, she can exercise "creative grant writing" and apply for both federal grants at the same time with modifications in the agency's mission and treatment philosophy. In writing these grants, she will have to downplay the agency's desperation for funding, disguise the agency's dislike for the treatment approaches, and "bend" service data to convince the funding source that ARCC is very qualified to provide the services.

Lori knows she can resolve the agency's lack of planning and fundraising in several years. She just needs time. Lori has just prepared two new mission statements for approval at the next board meeting, one medically oriented, and one criminal justice oriented. Nevertheless, she feels uneasy. Should she be very honest in her grant applications and significantly decrease the agency's chance for survival? Is it ethical to "stretch the truth" in order to get a grant to provide needed services? Don't grants always "stretch the truth" to make the agency look great? Wasn't she just stretching things a bit further than most grants? Is creative grant writing for survival unethical?

Questions

1. Does a good end (agency survival and services), justify questionable means (creative grant writing)? Is creative grant writing for survival unethical?

2. Is it common to stretch the truth in a grant application?

3. What role should the feelings of Lori's staff play in her decision?

4. What would you do if you were Lori?

CASE TWENTY-ONE

❧

Too Many Chiefs

Big Brothers and Sisters of Metro City, Inc. is a local, county-wide agency affiliated with a national parent organization and the local United Way. Its main goal is to pair volunteers with children who need a same-sex role model to provide some guidance and concern in lieu of a missing parent. It is governed by a Board of Directors who manage the affairs of the organization. The Board of Directors is made up of business people from the community, some of whom are retired and have been involved with the agency for a number of years.

The board has a number of standing committees which include: 1) Executive Committee: the officers of the board; 2) Finance and Funding: responsible for the fiscal affairs of the agency as well as fundraising; 3) Recruitment and Community Relations: public relations and attracting new members; 4) Program and Personnel: overseeing the program; 5) Planning and Evaluation; and 6) Nominating. There are forty board members, active and honorary, some of whom never attend meetings. Others are quite active and committed and come to every monthly meeting.

In addition to the Executive Director, the agency has a staff of six, and about 175 volunteers. For such a small agency, its structure tends to be very bureaucratic. Although there is not an extensive system of departments, there is a distinct division between service delivery and the business office. Advantages to this strict division include economy and efficiency due to the division of labor based on areas of expertise; disadvantages of the structure include

121

the possibility of ritualistic behavior leading to mediocre performance. Although the structure tends to be formal, due to the small
staff size of the agency, informal relationships are strong. All staff
interact with staff of other levels and also with the board. Communication between the Board and staff is encouraged and actually occurs. This is what caused the problem for Carolyn Hopkins.

Carolyn Hopkins is the new Executive Director at the agency.
She soon discovered the most powerful individuals on the board
in Big Brothers/Big Sisters: a select few who constitute a kind of
"inner circle". This inner circle includes the President of the Board,
a retired real estate broker; the Treasurer of the Board, a retired
CPA; and two members of the board, one is a priest, and the other
is a businessman who donates much time and materials to the
agency. This group consists of friends who also meet frequently to
play cards and engage in other social activities. In these informal
settings, they often discuss agency matters.

It is well known among staff in the agency that if you want to
do something all you have to do is get the approval or agreement of
these key board members. Staff members have used "influence" to
their advantage and had often "gone around" the previous Executive Director to the inner circle of board members when they wanted
changes in policies, wanted to start a new program, or get money
for something, including raises. This is a major reason the former
Director resigned, as she was not able to stop this pattern of behavior. She had confronted the board about undermining her authority
by approving raises without her consent or knowledge, to no avail.

The most influential board member, Charlie Johnson, has been
involved with the agency almost since its inception. Because of his
long-standing commitment to the agency and its programs, he is
highly respected by all the other board members and the staff. He
is a very effective fundraiser for the agency, and he also donates time
and even materials from his own business to the agency. Mr. Johnson
is at the core of the powerful "inner circle" that really makes the
major decisions at the agency. He takes a very proprietary attitude
toward the agency, it is his "baby". Since he owns his own business,
he has a lot of flexible time that he spends at the agency.

The problem is that he won't let Carolyn Hopkins do her job. It
isn't that he thinks she is incompetent, he actually thinks quite
highly of her and had pushed for her appointment as director. It is
just that he is used to being in control, and has a very difficult time
giving up decision-making powers to others. Carolyn was not aware

Big Mistake

of the events that had transpired before she took her position as Director. But she soon realized what was happening because staff continued to go around her to the board about issues that she believes are her decisions. Carolyn has many years of experience as a supervisor and administrator. She is used to the authority normally delegated by the board to the administrator.

About two months after she started her present job, two events occurred that made Carolyn realize she had to take a stand or find another job. The first event involved her Assistant Director, Stan Barnes. Stan had been assistant to the previous Director and had applied for the job as Director. He was somewhat bitter about not getting the Director's job, but felt he would try to make the best of it. Since he knew all the board members intimately, however, he knew he didn't have to go to the Director to ask her permission for anything. Therefore, he went to his friends on the board, and asked for and received one month's leave with pay for all his hard work as Acting Director. He then went to Carolyn and told her his leave had been approved, knowing that there was no money in the agency budget to hire a replacement for him.

The second event was that Cynthia Crumley, a Program Director, went to the board and asked for a raise without discussing it first with Carolyn. Carolyn found out about the request when it was put on the agenda for the next board meeting. Carolyn knew she had to act decisively.

Questions

who put the item on the agenda?

1. What steps should Carolyn take, if any, to prohibit staff from communicating with the board?

2. What steps should Carolyn take, if any, to inhibit board members from interfering with day-to-day operations of the agency?

3. What should be the relationship of staff to its board?

4. What are the underlying issues in this agency that have contributed to the current problems?

CASE TWENTY-TWO

ₔ

Staff Meetings at Senior Citizen Centers of the Valley, Inc.

Kathy Wallace felt more annoyed each minute as she sat listening to the droning voices of the Executive Director and Business Manager as they gave updates on the budget situation of the agency to the staff. She kept glancing at her watch, counting the minutes—the seconds—until she could flee the boring meeting. Kathy felt anxious because she kept thinking about all the work she had to do back at her desk: she had end of the month reports to be sent to the state, and clients to see. She didn't have time to sit and listen to these discussions that had little to do with her work. Indeed, she didn't see the point to them at all.

Staff meetings at Senior Citizen Centers of the Valley, Inc., seemed to be an ad hoc affair since she started working there a few months ago. The Executive Director, Estelle Logan, had once been Volunteer Coordinator at the agency. This was an important job as the agency depended on volunteers to perform many functions there. In fact, there were many more volunteers than staff at Senior Centers. Estelle had devoted much time to senior citizen issues and spent long hours at the agency filling in wherever she was needed. When the Executive Director position became available, everyone on the board naturally thought of offering her the job. As she was highly effective in the community as an advocate for seniors, it was felt that her visibility in the aging network would be an asset for the agency.

However, Estelle seemed to view her staff as tall children who needed to be looked after and nurtured. She took a very maternal approach to the staff, just as she had with the agency volunteers, bringing them snacks and sweets, sending them little notes, and remembering everyone's birthday. She knew what she wanted to do at the agency and had no use for what she termed "bureaucratic paraphernalia" such as agency policies and procedures manuals, job descriptions, or meeting minutes. Some of these materials were available, however, due to the efforts of the previous administrator.

There were regularly scheduled staff meetings twice a month that all professional staff were required to attend. No meeting agenda was distributed ahead of time, nor was one ever available at the meetings, so staff never knew what to expect. In addition, no minutes were ever taken at the meetings, so later there were often disagreements about what had actually transpired. Even if there were minutes, they would be of no consequence: the staff knew that Estelle's version of the meeting and any decisions made would prevail in any case.

Staff meetings were supposed to last 2 hours, but rarely ended on time. This often caused problems as the caseworkers had other appointments scheduled. Estelle never paid attention to the clock and became irritated when staff gradually drifted away from the meeting. She believed in process more than product, so anyone at the meeting could speak as long as they wished, on any topic. She thought it rude to interrupt and she thought it a reflection of her empathetic nature that she listened attentively to whomever was speaking.

Indeed, these staff meetings were meandering affairs with little substance. It seemed no important decisions were ever made there. If an important issue did arise, a sub-group would be formed to investigate it and report back at the next staff meeting. At that point, Estelle would either appoint another sub-group to investigate some esoteric aspect that was overlooked or she would table it.

It was also clear that *Robert's Rules of Order* were not used in these meetings, nor were any other guidelines. There were no motions, or seconds, or any other organized procedures. Estelle used the intuitive approach to try to reach consensus among the staff, or at least, Kathy ruminated, her version of consensus. It seemed that when Estelle did ask for votes on some issue, she always reserved what she called "administrative judgement." Therefore, if the vote did not go her way she would say that in any case it was an administrative decision and she would take the sentiment of the group into consideration. Staff seemed to accept this, being more concerned about their clients than the Director's administrative prerogatives.

Estelle knew the history of the agency in great detail as she had been there so long. Whenever an issue was brought up for discussion, she was very methodical in her approach. First, she explained the history of the issue and how it had been dealt with in the past; she always felt it was important to explain an issue's historical context. Then she presented a rationale for the procedure or issue at hand, defending it vehemently against all who would protest. Some of the other staff, including the Assistant Director and the Volunteer Coordinator, had been there as long as Estelle and supported her actions.

Kathy thought of the large multi-service agency, Hunt County Citizens in Action (HCCA), where she had worked before coming to Senior Centers. At the time she had not appreciated the smooth organization of the agency, but in retrospect she realized that the quiet competence of the Director had made running an agency look easy. Kathy had actually looked forward to the staff meetings at her old job. As a new social worker she found them stimulating learning experiences.

At HCCA staff meetings were very structured affairs. There was a planning committee that worked with the Executive Director to plan meetings for the whole year. All staff were on committees that were assigned specific tasks relating to the meetings. For example, one committee might be in charge of refreshments, another in charge of speakers, and so forth.

Since it was a large agency and people tended to stay in their own programs, the meetings were used to acquaint and update staff on the workings of the different programs. Every month, a different program or issue would be presented by various staff, then there would be general discussion of the presentation. There was also sharing of information about staff concerns, such as, health insurance, changes in laws regarding client rights, malpractice insurance, and so on.

Kathy had come to Senior Centers because she felt that she was ready to move up into a more responsible position. She had taken the job as Assistant Program Director because it seemed to be a good opportunity. She still carried a small caseload as well as some administrative duties. But the staff meetings here seemed to be such time wasters that she hated to attend them.

She looked around at others at the meeting. There was Joe Gorman, a new Program Director at one of the centers. He thought Estelle was an anachronism whose departure was long overdue. Joe knew that although Estelle was obviously not an effective administrator, she seemed to have the support of the board for her advocacy and ability at fundraising. Most of the caseworkers thought she served a useful function in her advocacy role but sorely lacked administrative skills, as was most evident in the staff meetings. Joe wrote a note and passed it down the table to Kathy. It read, "I've had it with these meetings. Let's meet in my office to see if we can come up with some ideas."

Most of the staff complained about these meetings. But Kathy wasn't sure what could be done to change them. Perhaps she should meet with Joe Gorman and some of the others to discuss it. But what if the Director found out? How would that affect Kathy's new position? As a new employee she was on probation for 6 months: thus, she was in a vulnerable position. She didn't have the longevity or the circle of support that some of the long-time staff had. Maybe she should just keep quiet like her colleague across the table, Steve Rosen, who seemed to have fallen asleep.

Questions
ᴥ

1. What should the role and purpose of staff meetings in human service agencies be?

2. What are some characteristics of well-run staff meetings?

3. What should the staff try to do about the Executive Director's style of leading staff meetings?

4. What would you do if you were in Kathy's position?

Index of Cases

Printed in the United States
154648LV00012B/19/A

9 780826 177414